Biblical Insights Into

'God's Chosen People'

plus
What Do You Mean, Truth?
and
The Role of Religion in America

Des Griffin

Copyright © 2001
Des Griffin Special Alert Newsletter
Box 294 Colton OR 97017
ISBN: 0-941380-08-4

All rights reserved. No part of this book may be reproduced in any form without permission in writing from the author, except by a reviewer who wishes to quote brief passages in connection with a review in a newspaper or magazine.

Table of Contents

Introduction	v.
Foreword	vi.
Honest Questions, But No Honest Answers	2.
"I Will Bless Them That Bless Thee"	3.
Two Covenants	3.
"All Came To Pass"	4.
Did the Curses "All Come To Pass"?	5.
Israel Broke the Covenant	6.
The Future Looked Grim	7.
Politically Astute	8.
Oblivious To Reality	8.
Daniel Had Knowledge and Understanding	10.
The Seventy Weeks Prophecy	12.
A Remnant Returned to Jerusalem	13.
Contradictory Prophecies?	14.
God Divorced Israel	15.
Jews Rejected Christ	16.
"Chosen People" in the New Testament?	17.
"I Am the Vine"	19.
Future of the Israel of God?	20.
God's Overview of Both Jew and Gentile	20.
You Must Be Born Again	22.
Brought Immortality to Light Through the Gospel	23.
A Simple But Profound Truth	25.
God's Chosen People — the "Israel of God"	26.
Most Don't Want To Be Confused With the Facts	26.
A Blatant Misapplication of God's Word	27.
Isaac and the Children of Promise	28.
Identifying "the Children of Promise"	31.
Romans Chapter Nine	32.
"The People Which He Foreknew"	32.
"God ... Hath Prepared For Them a City"	34.
Another "Hope"	35.

"If You Will Fall Down and Worship Me"	36.
A Strong Delusion	38.
"Jerusalem ... Mother of Us All"	38.

APPENDIX I — What Do You Mean, Truth? 40.

Garbage In, Garbage Out!	41.
Refusing To Deal With Reality	42.
"Great Is Diana of the Ephesians"	43.
Don't Confuse Me With the Facts	44.
Israeli-Palestinian Article	46.
What Do You Mean, Truth?	46.
Jewish Utopia	48.

APPENDIX II —
  What Is the Role of Religion in the 21st Century? 50.

Defining Terms	50.
Facing Reality	50.
Checking The Facts	51.
The Masonic Religion	53.
Who Is Masonry's Final Authority?	54.
Biblical Christianity	56.
Suffering From Bad Doctrine	57.
America Has Changed Its Religion	59.

Introduction

Des Griffin is the author of five other books: *Fourth Reich of the Rich* (1976); *Descent Into Slavery?* (1980); *Martin Luther King — The Man Behind the Myth* (1987); *Anti-Semitism and the Babylonian Connection* (1988), and *Storming the Gates of Hell* (1996).

Des Griffin is a long-time student of national and international affairs. He has written numerous articles on a wide variety of subjects, including history, politics, economics, and religion.

The fact that he has never been one to mince words or to refrain from calling a spade a spade, is amply demonstrated in the book you now hold in your hands. You may well find *God's Chosen People* to be one of the most challenging, thought-provoking, and enlightening publications you have ever read.

The author asks that you judge the contents of this text **exclusively** on its biblical merits — not by some undefined glandular reaction void of knowledge and understanding.

The **ONLY** intellectually honest criteria for acceptance or rejection of his basic premise must be: **Is it right ... or is it wrong?** Is this what God's Word truly teaches on this critical subject, or is it not? **No other standard is worthy of consideration.**

The reader is asked to carefully - and prayerfully — follow the sterling example of the Bereans in *Acts* 17:10-11: **With all readiness of mind, search the scriptures to see whether these things be so.**

If they are, then thankfully rejoice in the glorious truth contained in the pages of God's Word. If they are false, **PLEASE** write or call the author and calmly point out to him where he has misread, misquoted, misunderstood, or misrepresented the plain, spirit-breathed word of the Creator God. Consult a concordance. Check a Lexicon. Read. Think. Compare. "*Prove all things; hold fast that which is good*" (*I Thessalonians* 5:21). **Let God be true and every man a liar!**

As Henry Ford, the renowned auto pioneer, wrote early in the last century: "The truth frequently seems unreasonable, the truth frequently is depressing, the truth sometimes seems to be evil; but it has the eternal advantage, it is the truth, and what is built thereon neither brings nor yields to confusion."

Foreword

The spiritual insights revealed in this book are profound. They are revolutionary — in the truest spiritual sense of the word. If read, understood, acknowledged, proven true from the pages of God's Word, and applied in your life, they could be instrumental in eliminating many of the spiritual misconceptions — and mental cobwebs — that have proven so detrimental and debilitating over the years. They could transform your life — and make it truly meaningful!

But you — the reader of this book — may well have a problem. Although you may be totally sincere in what you presently believe, you may also be the unknowing victim of a religious belief system that has — perhaps unwittingly — led you astray in some crucial areas of knowledge and understanding.

The possibility exists that, while being totally sincere in your religious beliefs, you may be unknowingly wrong in some important areas. Sincerity is no criteria of right or wrong. One may be totally sincere and totally wrong at the same time. It happens all the time!

Is it remotely possible that the error you accept as "truth" may be stunting your spiritual growth, causing you numerous other problems?

Famed lawyer Gerry Spence makes an important point: "Peeping into a prejudiced mind is like opening the door to a room packed to the ceiling with junk. Nothing whatsoever can get in, and when the door opens, the junk comes tumbling out....

"Growth is dead. Learning is gridlocked.... People are prejudiced both for and against a philosophy, a religion, a belief system, a race, a person — you name it.... You can drown the prejudiced person in reason, scream, weep, and beg, but your pleas for fairness and justice will go for naught. You had just as well sing to a bag of jelly beans....

"The problem is that our prejudices may lie lurking at the bottom of the subterranean mind, where they slowly ooze up, and color our thinking without our knowing it...." (*How to Argue and Win Every Time*, pgs.74,75).

If you close *God's Chosen People* at this point, it will have something to do with your prejudice.

Biblical Insights Into
'God's Chosen People?'

Who programs your religious computer? Who controls your religious belief system? Who writes your religious 3 X 5 cards? God? Some respected religious "authority"? You? Do you really know and understand what you believe — and why? Come, let us reason together.

In recent decades millions of "men of God" — preachers and evangelists — have waxed eloquent on the subject of "God's Chosen People." There is almost unanimous agreement that "the Jews" hold that honor and distinction. To challenge this assumption is tantamount, in the minds of most, to inviting the wrath of Almighty God to come crashing down upon us with catastrophic results.

Any stated or implied criticism of "God's Chosen People" is therefore met with screaming howls of "Anti-Semitism." Perpetrators of such a "hate crime" are sometimes charged with being "rabid hate mongers." Interestingly and revealingly, these same people are deathly silent on the subject of the Jews' Talmudic hatred of Christ and his followers.

It is a biblical fact that Jesus Christ is God and that "all things were made by him, and without him was not any thing made that was made" (*John* 1:1-3). Jesus Christ, alone, is "**the** way, **the** truth, and **the** life" (*John* 14:6). How, then, do these same "men of God" reconcile the fact that "God's Chosen People" hate, despise, and abhor their Maker? Stop and think! Does there not seem to be something strange, peculiar, or ludicrous about this situation?

This unrelenting abhorrence by most religious Jews of the Lord Jesus Christ is laid out in no uncertain terms in their *Talmud* — "the ultimate authority" in Judaism (Article on "Judaism," *Encyclopedia Judaica*, p.396). There, Jesus is described as the bastard son of a woman "who played the whore with carpenters" (*Sanhedrin* 106b). The *Talmud* also tells us that Jesus was "a bloody and deceitful man" (*Gittin* 56b); that Jesus "was a fool and we pay no attention to what fools do" (*Sanhedrin* 65a). It also says that Jesus was "taken as one of the worst three enemies of Judaism" (*Gittin* 56b-57a). The *Talmud* also speaks of the "unforgivable sin of accepting Christianity." In fact, incest is considered a "light sin" compared to embracing Christianity (*Abodah Zarah*, 17a). Finally, the *Talmud* — unchallengeably the number one authority in Judaism — dogmatically declares that our Lord Jesus Christ, by whom "all things [were] created" ... and by whom "all things consist" (*Colossians* 1:16,17) **is presently "boiling in hot excrement"** (*Gittin* **56b**). He will, we are told, have "no portion in the world to come" (*Sanhedrin* x.2; 90a).

Jewish author Benjamin Freedman tells us that "**the *Talmud* exercises virtually totalitarian dictatorship over the lives of Jews whether they are aware of it or not**. Their spiritual leaders make no attempt to conceal the control they exercise over the lives of Jews. They extend their authority far beyond the legitimate limits of spiritual matters. Their authority has no limit outside religion" (*Facts Are Facts*, p.26).

In the light of such damning evidence, how can any professed "man of God" claim that a group which embraces such a virulent anti-Christ, anti-God philosophy can be "God's Chosen People"?

HONEST QUESTIONS, BUT NO HONEST ANSWERS

On a variety of occasions this writer has contacted preachers and evangelists seeking an answer to that and other related questions. We have yet to receive an honest answer — one that addresses the basic questions from a biblical perspective. Our enquiries have either been ignored, "answered" with insipid form letters, or met with childish, almost asinine charges of being "anti-semitic" or "lacking in love." We have also been told that people who ask such questions are "filled with bitterness and hate." Or that they are "aberrant individuals with an unhealthy obsession." Lots of name-calling, but no answers! Note well: The primary issue is **never** addressed. And the *New Testament* is **never** used to defend such a basically untenable position.

One Florida-based evangelist was particularly smug and self-righteous. He wrote: "We will not argue, we will not be angry, just love you and pray that you **also** will seek the Lord on this." **[Interpretation**: "We alone have sought the Lord on this matter. You obviously haven't. As we, in our awesome spirituality, are clearly much more righteous than you — you poor dumb, carnal minded, unspiritual slob — we don't have to address any of the issues you raise".]

The obvious purpose of such a conceited approach is to lay a guilt trip on any who ask questions, and thus avoid answering the queries from an honest, biblical perspective. It is clearly an attempt to win through intimidation. This is deceitful — and totally unworthy of anyone professing to be a Bible-believing Christian.

"I WILL BLESS THEM THAT BLESS THEE"

The current "chosen people" myth is based on a complete misunderstanding of scriptural truth. It begins with a hideous misinterpretation of *Genesis* 12:1-3, and goes downhill from there. Let's examine those verses: ""Now the Lord ... said to **ABRAM** [later Abraham] ... I will make of thee a great nation, and I will bless thee, and make thy name great, and thou shalt be a blessing.

"I will bless them that bless thee, and curse him that curseth thee, and **IN THEE** [Abraham] shall **all families [nations] of the earth be blessed....**"

A similar promise was made by God to Jacob, Abraham's grandson: "[A]nd in **thy seed** shall **all the families of the earth be blessed**" (*Genesis* 28:14). Notice that these specific promises concerning "all nations" and "all the families of the earth" were made in connection with other promises. As we shall see from scripture, some of these promises were physical in nature; others were spiritual. The former promises concerned **physical** blessings and advantages that would accrue to the Hebrew people (Israel) as a result of God's covenant blessings. The latter promises were **spiritual** in nature.

The latter promises are — and can only be — fulfilled in and through our Lord Jesus Christ. *This will soon become abundantly clear.*

TWO COVENANTS

It is a biblical fact that God chose the ancient Hebrews (physical Israel) to "be a special people unto himself, above all people that are upon the face of the earth" (*Deuteronomy* 7:6). This reality is confirmed in *I Chronicles* 16:13; *Psalm* 105:6; *Isaiah* 44:1. It was with **these** people that he entered into a covenant. The terms of that solemn agreement were clearly understood. That covenant was *physical* in nature; it was also **conditional**. (It was totally unlike the second covenant which was *spiritual* — and **unconditional**). Here are the terms:

"Now therefore, **IF** ye will **OBEY** my voice indeed, and **KEEP** my covenant, **THEN** ye shall be *a peculiar treasure* unto me above **ALL** people: **FOR** all the earth is mine" (*Exodus* 19:5).

The "blessings" and "curses" of the first covenant are clearly laid out in the twenty-eighth chapter of *Deuteronomy*: "It **shall** come to pass, **IF** thou shalt hearken diligently unto the voice of the Lord thy God, to observe and to do **ALL** his commandments ... **that** the Lord thy God will set thee on high above all nations of the earth.

"And **all these blessings** shall come on thee, and overtake thee, **IF thou shalt hearken unto the voice of the Lord thy God**" (verse 1). In the next thirteen verses God enumerates spectacular blessings that would be literally piled upon Israel from every direction. Every phase and facet of their society would prosper almost beyond belief. Theirs would be a Utopian society.

Verse 14 contains a stern warning: "And **thou shalt NOT go aside from ANY of the words which I command thee this day**, to the right hand, or to the left, to go after other gods to serve them."

"B U T ..." Notice the big "BUT" at the beginning of verse 15. "**BUT** it **shall** come to pass, **IF** thou wilt **NOT** hearken unto the voice of the Lord thy God, to observe to do **ALL** his commandments and statutes which I command thee this day; that **all these curses shall come upon thee, and overtake thee....**"

These "curses" — and the results thereof — are enumerated in no uncertain terms in verses 16 through 68. Read them for yourself. The **conditions** of the physical covenant with Israel were clearly laid out. There was no room for misunderstanding. It was decreed by God that the end results of rebellion and covenant-breaking would be devastating. Israel would lose everything.

But before addressing that issue, let's deal with another important question.

"ALL CAME TO PASS"

How about all the marvelous **physical blessings** God promised to pour out upon physical Israel? Did the Creator "come through" as promised — or was he tardy in their fulfillment? Instead of going to some wild-eyed, agenda-promoting, Bible-thumping, religious zealot with an axe to grind to have that question answered, let's hear the clear, unequivocal testimony of Joshua, Israel's commander-in-chief. He was the man under whom the covenant-keeping Creator God brought Israel into the promised land following Moses' death approximately 1450 B.C. (*Joshua*, chapter 1).

"**And the Lord gave** unto Israel **ALL** the land which he sware to give unto their fathers; and **they possessed it, and dwelt therein**.

"**And the Lord gave them rest round about**, according to **ALL** that he sware unto their fathers: and there stood **not** a man of **ALL** their enemies before them; **the Lord** delivered **ALL** their enemies into their hand.

"There **failed not ought** of **any** good thing which **the Lord** had spoken unto the house of Israel; **ALL came to pass**" (*Joshua* 21:43-45).

It may be asked, somewhat facetiously: What part of "**ALL**" is it that some "Bible students" seem incapable of understanding? It should be noted that seven is a biblical number of completeness. As God wanted to clearly convey the message that **ALL** his promises of physical blessings to Israel had been completely fulfilled, he inspired Joshua to say it **seven different ways**.

DID THE CURSES "ALL COME TO PASS"?

The history of ancient Israel is a sad one. It is replete with examples that emphasize the biblical fact that "every imagination of the thoughts of [man's] heart is only evil continually" (*Genesis* 6:5). Also, that "the heart is deceitful above all things and desperately wicked: who can know it?" (*Jeremiah* 17:9). That crucial issue was **not** dealt with under the terms of the old covenant. It **is**, thank God, perfectly dealt with under the new covenant.

Almost as soon as they came into the "promised land" under Joshua, the Israelites resumed their rebellious ways. Under their God-given judges they were never satisfied. Because of their naturally evil and rebellious hearts they seemed incapable of learning from their experiences — their trials and tribulations. As a result, after some 350 years the elders of Israel went to Samuel — a judge and prophet, and a true man of God — with an amazing demand: "Behold, thou art old, and thy sons walk not in thy ways; **make us a king to judge us like all the nations**" (*I Samuel* 8:5).

The Israelites weren't satisfied with being a "peculiar treasure" unto God. They didn't want the personal responsibility of being directly accountable to God. They didn't want a theocracy (in which God makes the rules); they wanted a form of "democracy" (in which man makes the rules). Yes, they wanted to be just like the Godless nations by which they were surrounded.

Samuel brought the problem to God. Notice God's answer: "Hearken unto the voice of the people in all that they say unto thee: **for they have not rejected thee, but they have rejected me, that I should rule over them**" (vs. 6-7).

God then warned Israel of the catastrophic consequences that would result. But Israel ignored the stern warning: "Nay, but **we will** [Notice, they were self-willed] have a king over us; **that we also may be like all the nations**; that **our** king may judge us, and go out before us, and fight our battles" (vs.19-20). After just three kings — Saul, David and Solomon — the kingdom broke up into warring factions and went from bad to worse, ending in slavery.

The six books of *Samuel*, *Kings*, and *Chronicles* record the generally sordid history of the kings of Israel. Though God had **chosen** Israel to be "a special people unto himself, above all people that are upon the face of the earth" (*Deuteronomy* 7:6), **the people chose** to reject the offer.

ISRAEL BROKE THE COVENANT

Some claim that God's physical covenant with Israel is eternal and is thus still in effect. They maintain that, as it is "impossible for God to lie" (*Hebrews* 6:18), his covenant with Israel must still be in effect. In saying that, they ignore a critical truth — the conditional nature of that covenant.

As God is totally faithful in all the covenants he makes (*I Kings* 8:23; *II Chronicles* 6:14; *Nehemiah* 1:5; *Psalm* 89:34), he couldn't break his word. Your Bible shows clearly that it was Israel which broke the covenant: "[T]he **children of Israel have forsaken thy covenant**, thrown down thine altars, and slain thy prophets with the sword" (*I Kings* 19:10). "**They kept not the covenant of God**, and refused to walk in his law" (*Psalm* 78:10). "[T]**hey were disobedient, and**

rebelled against thee, and cast thy law behind their backs, and slew thy prophets which testified against them to turn them to thee, and **they wrought great provocations"** (*Nehemiah* 9:26). **Israel "mocked the messengers of God, and despised his words, and misused his prophets, until the wrath of the Lord arose against his people, TILL THERE WAS NO REMEDY"** (*II Chronicles* 36:15-16)

Till there was no remedy! Enough was enough! Following Solomon's death came a break-up of the kingdom — and a continual rivalry between the northern and southern kingdoms of Israel and Judah. This animosity lasted until Israel was taken captive by the Assyrians following the fall of Samaria in 722 BC. Judah survived precariously for over a century before collapsing under the combined weight of God's displeasure and Nebuchadnezzar's armies. Thus began the Babylonian Captivity.

THE FUTURE LOOKED GRIM

The future looked grim, even hopeless. Centuries of stiffnecked rebellion and wilful disobedience had "paid off" exactly as the Creator God, through his prophets, had specifically stated they would. The Hebrew people — Israel and Judah — were now grovelling at the feet of their enemies in abject slavery.

Among the slaves initially dragged across the burning desert into captivity in Babylon was a young man, probably a teenager, named Daniel. He belonged to a noble — possibly royal — family, and was particularly capable and intelligent.

In his book of *Daniel*, the author emerges first as a statesman, then as a prophet. Throughout the book it is clear that Daniel and a few close companions knew their God — and were confident in their personal covenant relationship with their Creator. Understanding that his name meant "God is judge," it came as no great surprise to Daniel that his people ended up in captivity. He knew that Judah — having sneered and jeered at the dire warnings issued by God's prophet Jeremiah over the previous few decades — was now suffering the consequences. He matter-of-factly reports that, as a result of their disobedience, "the Lord gave Jehoiakim king of Judah into his [Nebuchadnezzar's] hand, with part of the vessels of the house of God, which he carried into the land of Shinar to the house of his god" (*Daniel* 1:2).

POLITICALLY ASTUTE

The king of Babylon was psychologically and politically astute. He implemented a strategy that "worked like a charm" with most of the captives. Having initially brought the cream of Judah's intellectual crop to Babylon, he changed their names (*Daniel* 1:7) and enrolled them in the Babylonian "education" system (1:4) that was dominated by "magicians, astrologers, and ... sorcerers" (2:2). He wanted to ensure their "political correctness."

As names and their meanings were extremely important to the Jewish people, the name changes imposed on them by Nebuchadnezzar were also very important. The new Babylonian names were part of a brainwashing program. The captives were required to participate in religious and political indoctrination programs designed to take their minds off their true purpose in life — so that they could be used in the furtherance of the Babylonian empire. The king wanted them to eventually become identified with the Babylonian world view. As it turned out, his program was largely successful.

Daniel's name means "God is judge." Nebuchadnezzar changed it to Belteshazzar, which means "protect the king's life." Hananiah's name, which means "God is gracious," was changed to Shadrack, meaning "circuit of the sun." Mishael, "favored by Jehovah," was changed to Meshack, possibly meaning "who is what Aku [the Chaldean god] is?" Azariah, "God has helped," had his name changed to Abednego, possibly meaning "servant of Nego [a Chaldean god]" (*Daniel* 1:6,7).

OBLIVIOUS TO REALITY

In their natural carnality and rebelliousness, most of the newcomers ignored the many graphic lessons embodied in the trials and tribulations experienced by their ancestors in centuries past. They were still oblivious to reality. They had learned nothing.

God's prophet Jeremiah had for decades warned Israel of the dire consequences of their rejection of God's covenant promises: "Hear now this, **O foolish people, and without understanding; which have eyes, and see not; which have ears, and hear not....**

"**Fear ye not me: will ye not tremble at my presence...?**

"But **this people hath a revolting and rebellious heart**; they have revolted and gone;

"Neither say they in their hearts, Let us now fear the Lord our God" (*Jeremiah* 5:21,22,23,24).

In this deplorable spiritual condition they were unable to "see" and understand the stark reality of the warning God delivered through his prophet: "Thus saith the LORD of hosts, the God of Israel, of Ahab the son of Zedekiah the son of Masseiah, which prophesy a lie unto you in my name: Behold, **I will deliver them into the hand of Nebuchadrezzar king of Babylon**, and he shall slay them before your eyes" (*Jeremiah* 29:21).

A few chapters later, Jeremiah elaborated: "**And thou shalt not escape out of his hand, but shall surely be taken, and delivered into his hand**; and thine eyes shall behold the eyes of the king of Babylon, and he shall speak to thee mouth to mouth, **and thou shalt go to Babylon**" (34:3).

In their "unseeing" and "unhearing" spiritual stupor that resulted from their refusal to let God rule over them, the Jewish slaves were captivated by what they encountered in Babylon. They were drawn like a magnet to the occult mysticism that prevailed in their new environment. Having previously worshipped and served false gods — and having formerly participated in all types of idolatry and demon worship — most felt perfectly at home in Babylon.

In Babylon, they embraced with wholehearted abandon numerous practices forbidden by God: "There shall **not** be found among you any that maketh his son or daughter to pass through the fire, or that useth divination ... or an enchanter, or a witch, or a charmer, or a consulter with familiar spirits, or a wizard, nor a necromancer. **For all that do these things are an abomination unto the LORD**" (*Deuteronomy* 18:10-12). Jewish history records that their "most profound scholars were adept in the black arts" ("Magic," *Jewish Encyclopedia*, p.255).

As time passed, it can truthfully be stated that many of the captives became more "Babylonian" than the Babylonians themselves. In the centuries to come the Jews were to be instrumental in developing the occult practices of Babylon and in spreading that corrupt system to the furthest corners of the globe. As a top Jewish authority points out, after 658 AD "**Babylonia was the spiritual center of Judaism**, and its influence brought many Babylonian customs into general use ("Babylonia," *Universal Jewish Encyclopedia*, pp.16-17).

At that moment in history — with both Israel and Judah crushed under the iron heel of tyrants — hopes of the promised Messiah appeared slim indeed. **This was undoubtedly the lowest point thus far in the history of the Hebrew people. The future looked bleak!**

But the faithful remnant were not in despair. They knew the Sovereign God was on his throne, ruling his universe, working out his divine plan. Besides, God's faithful prophet Jeremiah had earlier declared that they would "serve the king of Babylon seventy years" *(Jeremiah 25:11)*.

The remnant were further comforted by the fact that God, through Jeremiah, had proclaimed that **"it shall come to pass, when seventy years are accomplished, that I will punish the king of Babylon, and that nation ... for their iniquity ... and will make it perpetual desolations"** (25:12). A few chapters later: "Thus saith the LORD, that **after seventy years be accomplished at Babylon I will visit you, and perform my good word toward you, in causing you to return to this place [Jerusalem]"** (29:10).

DANIEL HAD KNOWLEDGE AND UNDERSTANDING

Daniel and his companions were different from the enslaved masses of Judah. They were part of a small remnant which remained faithful to the God of Abraham, Isaac and Jacob. They steadfastly refused to be corrupted by Babylonian customs. As a result, "God gave them knowledge and skill in all learning and wisdom; and Daniel had understanding in all visions and dreams" *(Daniel 1:17)*. Daniel was thus in a unique position to be used by God to encourage and inspire his compatriots when needed.

One such occasion arose when the king had a dramatic dream — one that startled and troubled him greatly. Claiming that the dream was "gone from me," he summoned his top advisers, demanding that they must not only tell him what he had just dreamed, but also give him the interpretation thereof. The king promised "gifts and reward, and great honor" to whoever could satisfy his demands (2:6). To the Babylonian "wise men" this was utterly impossible: "There is not a man upon the earth that can shew the king's matter; therefore there is no king, lord, nor ruler, that asked such things at any magician, or astrologer, or Chaldean.

"And it is a rare thing that the king requireth, and there is none other that can shew it before the king, except the gods, whose dwelling is not with flesh" (vs.10-11),

When they couldn't comply with his demands, the king was "angry and very furious" and issued a decree to "destroy all the wise men of Babylon" (v.12).

At this juncture, Daniel learned of the king's proclamation. Though not directly involved in angering the king, Daniel's head was on the line. He was listed among "all the wise men."

Asking for time, "Daniel went to his house, and made the thing known to Hananiah, Mishael, and Azariah, his companions" (v.17). Having asked God to reveal "this secret" to them, knowledge of the dream and its interpretation came to Daniel in a night vision (vs.28,29).

Going through Arioch, whom the king had commissioned to destroy the wise men of Babylon, Daniel gained access to king Nebuchadnezzar. Pointing out the lack of knowledge and understanding possessed by the king's magicians and astrologers, Daniel declared that **"there is a God in heaven that revealeth secrets**, and maketh known unto king Nebuchadnezzar what shall be in the latter days" (vs.27,28). Daniel went on to reveal that the king had seen "a great image, whose brightness was excellent.... This image's head was of fine gold, his breast and his arms of silver, his belly and his thighs of brass.

"His legs of iron, his feet part of iron and part of clay" (vs.31-33).

Daniel interpreted the dream. Nebuchadnezzar, he was inspired to reveal, was the head of gold. His kingdom "of fine gold" would topple, and be followed by an inferior one symbolized by "silver." A third "brass" empire would then take over. This, in turn, would give way to one "part iron and part clay." [Chronologically, these correspond to Babylon, Medo-Persia, Greece, and Rome].

It was then revealed to Daniel that "in the days of these kings **shall the God of heaven** [the God of Abraham, Isaac, and Jacob] **set up a kingdom which shall never be destroyed**: and the kingdom **shall not** be left to other people [human beings], but it **shall** break in pieces and consume all these kingdoms, and it **shall** stand for ever" (v.44). **In a striking metaphor, we are assured that as a result of the activities of this kingdom the Babylonian system would be "blown away"** (2:35).

The faithful remnant in captivity in Babylon were thus encouraged in their dedicated and obedient walk before God. All was not lost. God was still on his throne — working out his sovereign will among the nations of the world. **The remnant knew help was on the way.**

They also remembered the divine promise of redemption delivered earlier through Jeremiah: **"For thus saith the Lord. That after seventy years be accomplished at Babylon I will visit you, and perform my good word upon you**, in causing you to return to this place [Jerusalem]" (*Jeremiah* 29:10). Also: **"And it shall come to pass when seventy years are accomplished, that I will punish the king of Babylon, and that nation, saith the LORD, for their iniquity, and the land of the Chaldeans, and will make it perpetual desolations"** (25:12). The message to the remnant was clear: Hang in there. Help is on the way.

The remnant knew the "writing was on the wall" for Babylon (5:5). It had been "weighed in the balance and found wanting" (5:25-27). The head of "gold" was shortly to bite the dust. Its fate was sealed.

THE SEVENTY WEEKS PROPHECY

The years roll by. The captivity continues. The date is 538 B.C. The prophesied seventy years is nearing its end. At this juncture Daniel pours out his heart to God: "O Lord, the great and dreadful God, keeping the covenant and mercy of them that love him, and to them that keep his commandments.

"We have sinned and committed iniquity, and have done wickedly, and have rebelled, even by departing from thy precepts and from thy judgments....

"Yea, all Israel have transgressed thy law ... the curse is poured upon us ... because we have sinned against him" (*Daniel* 9:4,5,11).

In verse 19 Daniel concludes his confession of national sin and prays for mercy on behalf of his people: **"O Lord, hearken and do; defer not, for thine own sake, O my God; for thy city and thy people are called by thy name."**

This prayer was centered exclusively on God's covenant promise to bless all nations through the seed of Abraham.

Around this time Gabriel (identified in *Luke* 1:19,26 and *Daniel* 8:16 as an angelic messenger of God) appeared to Daniel with a vital message: "**O Daniel, I am now come forth to give thee skill and understanding.**

"At the beginning of thy supplications the commandment came forth, and I am come to shew thee; **for thou art greatly beloved**; therefore understand the manner and consider the vision" (*Daniel* 9:22,23).

What followed is almost certainly the most amazing, succinct, detailed prophecy in all of scripture: "Seventy weeks are determined upon thy people and upon thy holy city, [A] to finish the transgressions, and [B] to make an end of sins, and [C] to make reconciliation for iniquity, and [D] to bring in everlasting righteousness, and [E] to seal up the vision and prophecy, and [F] to anoint the most Holy" (*Daniel* 9:24).

"**Know therefore and understand**, that from the going forth of the commandment to restore and build Jerusalem, **unto the Messiah the Prince** shall be seven weeks, and three score and two weeks: the street shall be built again, and the wall, even in troublous times" (v.25).

"And after three score and two weeks shall Messiah be cut off, but **not** for himself: and the people of the prince shall come and shall destroy the city and the sanctuary; and the end thereof shall be with a flood, and unto the end of the war desolations are determined" (v.26).

"And **he shall confirm the covenant** with many for one week; and in the midst of the week shall cause the sacrifice and the oblation to cease, and for the overspreading of abominations he shall make it desolate, even unto the consummation. and that determined shall be poured upon the desolate" (v.27).

Lack of space prevents a full, detailed explanation of how each of the events prophesied to occur during the seventieth weeks of Daniel's remarkable prophecy were fulfilled in perfect detail during the ministry of our Lord Jesus Christ. The reader will find this detailed and thoroughly documented information in chapter 16 of this author's book, *Storming the Gates of Hell*.

A REMNANT RETURNED TO JERSUSLEM

Daniel was in Babylon when the forces of Cyrus, the Persian, captured that city. He was a high government official during the reign of Cyrus (539-529 B.C.) and Cambyses (529-522 B.C.). He served also during his old age under the reign of Darius I, the son of Hystaspes (522-486 B.C.).

After seventy years of captivity, under a proclamation issued by Cyrus, a small **remnant** providentially returned to Jerusalem under Ezra and Nehemiah (See *II Chronicles* 36:22; *Ezra* 1:1-3). This opened up the way for the fulfillment of the prediction made in *Genesis* 49:10: "The scepter ["A staff borne by kings.... Royal power and authority," Webster] shall **not** depart from Judah, nor a lawgiver from between his feet, **until** Shiloh [Christ the Messiah] come, **and unto him shall the gathering of the people be**"("the people" are "the [singular] people of God" mentioned in *I Peter* 2:9,10). With the arrival of Christ, Judah had fulfilled its divine mission.

CONTRADICTORY PROPHECIES?

King Jehoiakim, who was a captive in Babylon, was the last occupant of the throne of David in the direct line from father to son. At the time Jehoiakim was carried away to Babylon, the prophet Jeremiah made two prophecies that initially appear to contradict each other. In chapter 22, God declares through Jeremiah: "**As I live saith the Lord, though Coniah, son of Jehoiakim king of Judah were the signet upon my right hand, yet would I pluck thee thence.**

"And I will give thee ... into the hand of Nebuchadnezzar king of Babylon, and into the hand of the Chaldeans (vs.24,25).

"Is this man Coniah a despised broken idol? Is he a vessel wherein there is no pleasure? Wherefore are they cast out, he and his seed, and are cast into a land which they knew not?....

"Thus saith the Lord, **Write ye this man childless, a man that shall not prosper in his days; for no man of his seed shall prosper, sitting upon the throne of David, and ruling any more in Judah**" (vs.28,30).

A later prophecy appears — at first glance — to say the exact opposite: "**David shall never want a man to sit upon the throne of the House of Israel....** Thus saith the Lord, If ye can break my covenant of the day and my covenant of the night, and that there should not be day and night in their season; **then may also my covenant be broken with David my servant, that he should not have a man to reign upon his throne**" (*Jeremiah* 33:17-21).

For a succinct analysis of how the royal line was preserved, we quote from famous Christian author, Philip Mauro: "It is a matter of deepest interest to trace the complete fulfillment of both these lines of prophecy concerning David and his house, prophecies which seem on their face to contradict each other.

"The genealogy of the royal line was carefully preserved and is given in *Matthew* 1, from Abraham and David (the two Old Testament pillars of the Gospel) to Joseph, the betrothed husband of Mary, of whom Christ was born. This line runs through Jehoiachin, but according to the Word of God, in *Jeremiah* 22:30, no man of his seed was to sit upon the throne of David or rule anymore in Judah. This word, however, does not bar Jesus Christ, for He was not "of the seed" of Jehoiachin, being born of a virgin, the Seed of the woman. But He was born under the roof of Joseph, the son of Jeconiah, the heir to the throne, and of one whom Joseph had betrothed to himself as his wife. Hence, under the law of Israel, He was entitled to the throne.

"The other prophecy, which pledged the throne to David's seed forever, is also fulfilled in that Mary, the mother of Jesus Christ, was of the house of David, *but her descent* (given in Luke 3) *does not come through Jeconia* and the other kings of Judah, but through David's son Nathan, the younger brother of Solomon, Nathan also being a son of Bathsheba (*I Chronicles* 3:5)" [*The Wonders of Bible Chronology* (2001 edition), p.96].

Since that time God has worked exclusively with a remnant (*Romans* 9:27), a little flock (*Luke* 12:32), an elect (*Colossians* 3:12), a chosen people (*I Peter* 2:9).

GOD DIVORCED ISRAEL

Through the prophet *Jeremiah*, God declared that, by breaking the covenant, "**backsliding Israel committed adultery, I had put her away, and given her a bill of divorce; yet her treacherous daughter Judah feared not, but went and played the harlot also**" (3:8).

Later, Judah also was divorced. These divorces were finalized when, at Christ's crucifixion, "the veil of the temple was rent in twain from the top to the bottom" (*Matthew* 27:51). God had departed from the temple in Jerusalem. The old covenant was "done away in Christ" (*II Corinthians* 3:14). Through Jesus Christ a glorious new, life-changing, world-changing covenant was thus established.

Jesus Christ "by himself purged our sins [and] sat down on the right hand of the Majesty on high" (*Hebrews* 1:3). Jesus Christ is now our "advocate" (*I John* 2:1) and "mediator" (*I Timothy* 2:5) so that "**they** which are called might receive the promise of eternal inheritance" (*Hebrews* 9:15b). This **new** covenant is sealed in the blood of the Lord Jesus Christ. Access to the Father — **for those who are called** — is now exclusively through the Lord Jesus Christ. "Neither is there salvation in **any** other: **for there is none other name under heaven given among men, whereby we must be saved**" (*Acts* 4:12).

Man, with his natural "carnal mind, **IS** enmity [bitterness, hatred and hostility] against God ... [He] is **NOT** subject to the law of God, **neither indeed CAN be**" (*Romans* 8:7). He just doesn't have the ability. It should be abundantly obvious, therefore, that no man **CAN** do anything to "save" himself spiritually. Salvation "is the **GIFT** of God; **NOT** of works [anything that man can do] **lest any man should boast**" (*Ephesians* 2:8-9).

As Jesus clearly stated, "**NO MAN CAN** come to me, **EXCEPT** the Father which hath sent me **DRAW** him" (*John* 6:44). In the same chapter, Jesus elaborated, "[N]o man **CAN** come unto me, **EXCEPT** it were **GIVEN** unto him by my Father" (v. 65).

Under the new covenant God is the only **active** party; the people involved are strictly **passive**. "**I** [singular] will put **my** laws in **their** inward parts, and write it in their hearts; and will be their God, and **they shall be my people**... [T]hey shall all **know** me [have a close, intimate relationship with me]... **I will forgive their iniquity, and remember their sins no more**" (*Jeremiah* 31:31-34. Also *Hebrews* 9:10).

Under the new covenant, Jesus Christ does **not** "offer" people redemption; **he gives it to them**. It's unconditional — an act of Sovereign Grace!

JEWS REJECTED CHRIST

During Jesus' earthly ministry, "the common people heard him gladly" (*Mark* 12:37). But the religious leaders of Israel were in open rebellion against the one who is "the way, the truth, and the life" (*John* 14:6). They despised him, spread lies about him, plotted to kill him. Their virulent hatred of the Lord Jesus Christ knew no bounds.

Jesus' reaction is recorded in *Matthew* 23. He condemned them as hypocrites, blind fools, a generation of vipers. He knew God was about to wrap up his covenant with physical Israel, and lower the curtain on the whole sordid scene. Upon them would "**come all the righteous** blood shed upon the earth, from the blood of righteous Abel unto the blood of Zacharias....

"Verily I say unto you, ALL these things shall come upon THIS generation.

"O Jerusalem, Jerusalem, thou that killest the prophets and stoned them that were sent unto you, *how often would I have gathered your children together even as a hen gathereth her chicks under her wings, and* ye would not.

"Behold, YOUR house [the "house" they had built on a false foundation, *Luke* 6:49] **is left unto you desolate**" (*Matthew* 23:35-38).

After Christ's death, resurrection, and ascension into heaven, the Apostle Paul — a Pharisee who had "made havoc of the church" before his miraculous conversion on the road to Damascus (*Acts* 8:3) — mightily preached the gospel. The Jewish leaders accused him of being "a pestilent fellow ... a mover of sedition ... and a ringleader of the sect of the Nazarenes" (*Acts* 24:5). They wanted to kill him also.

In the book of *Deuteronomy*, the Sovereign God stated that one of the results of Israel's (and Judah's) incessant rebellion would be a descent into cannibalism: "**And thou shalt eat the fruit of thine own body, the flesh of thy sons, and of thy daughters**, which the Lord thy God hath given thee, in the siege and in the straitness, wherewith thine enemies shall distress thee" (*Deuteronomy* 28:53).

Jewish historian Flavius Josephus records that this prediction was fulfilled during Rome's siege of Jerusalem, 66-70 A.D: "O most wretched city, what misery so great as this didst thou suffer from the Romans, when they came to purify thee from thine intestine hatred! For thou couldst be no longer a place fit for God, nor couldst thou continue in being, after thou hadst been a sepulchre for the bodies of thine own people, and hadst made the holy house itself a burying place for this civil war of thine. Yet mayest thou again grow better, if perchance thou wilt hereafter appease the anger of that God who is the author of thy destruction" (*The Works of Flavius Josephus*, p. 773, International Press, Philadelphia).

"CHOSEN PEOPLE" IN THE NEW TESTAMENT?

It is obvious from the above scriptures that the followers of occult Talmudic Judaism cannot be thought of as "God's chosen people." Jesus clearly stated that they were "of [their] father the Devil" (*John* 8:44).

God is now working in and through another type of people, another type of nation: **Spiritual Israel**. By the grace of God, spiritual Israel is comprised of "a great multitude, which no man can number, from **all nations**, and kindreds, and people, and tongues... [who are] clothed with white robes..." *(Revelation* 7:9). They are the recipients of God's promise that, in Abraham's seed [Jesus Christ], **all nations** of the earth would be blessed.

"Impossible," say many. "The Jews alone are Abraham's seed ... his chosen people." Anything else is "damnable heresy."

Let's check the scriptures: "Now to **Abraham and his seed** were the promises made. He saith **not**, And to **seeds** [plural], as of many; but as of **one** [singular], **And to thy seed [singular], which is Christ....**"

"And **IF** ye be Christ's, **Then are ye [Gentiles] Abraham's SEED**, and heirs according to the promise" *(Galatians* 3:16,29).

"The **blessing of Abraham** [came] on the **Gentiles through Jesus Christ**; that [they] might receive the promise of the Spirit through faith" (v.14).

How does one become "Christ's" — a member of Spiritual Israel?

"But **ye** are a **chosen** generation, a royal priesthood, a holy nation, a peculiar people [remember *Exodus* 19:5, *a peculiar treasure ...* above **ALL** people?] that ye should show forth the praises of **him who has called you out of** darkness **into** his marvelous light:

"Which **in time past** were **not** a people, **but are now the [singular] people of God**... *(I Peter* 2:9,10).

"**Ye have NOT chosen me, but I have chosen you**," said Jesus Christ *(John* 15:16). But of course! True Christians are **not** the choosing people, **they are the chosen people.** They did not "make a decision for Christ." Just as they didn't decide to be born the first time of human parents, they didn't decide to be "born again" spiritually. **Jesus Christ made that decision for them**. They did not "give their hearts to the Lord." The Lord gave his life for them. Jesus Christ "quickeneth [makes spiritually alive] whom **HE** will" *(John* 5:21). That decision was made "**before the foundation of the world that we should be holy and without blame before him in love**" *(Ephesians* 1:4). The names of God's elect — Jew and Gentile alike — were "written in the book of life of the Lamb before the foundation of the world" *(Revelation* 13:8).

"They which are **the children of the flesh** [physical Israel] **are NOT the children of God: but the children of promise ARE counted for**

'GOD'S CHOSEN PEOPLE'

the seed" (*Romans* 9:8). Children of promise? These people were **dead** (extinct, lifeless, insensitive, inanimate) **in their trespasses and sins** (*Ephesians* 2:1). No amount of artificial resuscitation could help them. They are the people who are **saved by God** because it was impossible for them to make a decision to be "born again" (*John* 3:3). **By grace are they saved** through faith; and that **not of themselves. It is the gift of God** (*Ephesians* 2:8). The new birth is the exclusive work of a Sovereign God.

Thus is fulfilled a wonderful Old Testament prophecy: "**I will say to my people which were NOT my people ... you are my people ...** (*Hosea* 2:23. See also *Romans* 9:24.25).

"For he is **not** a Jew who is one outwardly; **neither** is that circumcision, which is outward in the flesh.

"But he **is** a Jew who is one **inwardly**; and **circumcision is that of the heart**, in the spirit, and **not** in the letter; whose praise is **not** of men, **but of God**" (*Romans* 2:28,29).

This miraculous change of heart is totally supernatural — exclusively God's doing. When we are born again God puts **HIS** law in **our** inward parts, and writes it in our hearts. At that time **he becomes our God, and we become his people.** He forgives our iniquities, and remembers our sins no more (*Jeremiah* 31:31-34. Also *Hebrews* 8:10). Under the new covenant, the Sovereign God does **not** "offer" people redemption; **he gives it to them. It is God's good pleasure to GIVE the kingdom to his elect** (*Luke* 12:32). He predestined them unto the adoption of children by Jesus Christ unto himself, "**according to the good pleasure of his will**" (*Ephesians* 1:5). He has "made known unto [them] the mystery of his will, according to **his good pleasure which he has purposed in himself**" (*Ephesians* 1:9). "[I]t is God which worketh in [his people] **to will and to do of his good pleasure**" (*Philippians* 2:13). When the "eyes of our understanding" are enlightened we can then "know what is the hope of his calling and what the riches of the glory of his inheritance in the saints" (*Ephesians* 1:18).

"I AM THE VINE"

In the *Old Testament* Israel is portrayed as a vine (*Psalm* 80:8,14-15; *Isaiah* 5:2,5). In *Jeremiah* we read that **Israel was "planted a noble vine ... but turned into a degenerate plant of a *strange* vine unto me [God]**" (2:21). That vine was rejected. In the *New Testament* Jesus reveals the identity of the new, true vine ("**the Israel of God**," *Galatians* 6:16):

"**I am the true vine** ... Abide in me and I in you. **As the branch cannot bear fruit of itself except it abide in the vine; no more can ye except ye abide in me.** I am the vine, ye are the branches" (*John* 15: 1,4,5).

Those who are Christ's are now the temple of the Holy Spirit (*I Corinthians* 6:19). "**For it is God which worketh in us to will and to do** of **HIS** good pleasure" (*Philippians* 2:13; also *Ephesians* 1:5,9). Christ in them is their hope of glory (*Colossians* 1:27).

FUTURE OF THE ISRAEL OF GOD?

"And we know that all things work together for them that love God, **to them that are THE called according to his purpose.**

"For whom **he** did foreknow, **he also did predestine to be conformed to the image of his Son**...

"**Moreover,** whom **he** did predestine, them **he** also called; and whom **he** called them **he** also justified; and whom **he** justified, them **he** also glorified" (*Romans* 8:28-30).

Could anything be clearer? Hardly! The Bible is abundantly clear. Salvation is by **GRACE, NOT RACE!** Did God possibly make a mistake? Paul answers: "O man, who art thou that repliest against God; **shall the thing formed say to him that formed it, Why hast thou made me thus?**

"**Hast not the potter power over the clay, of the same lump to make one vessel unto honor and another unto dishonour?**" (*Romans* 9:20,21).

There is no need for Christians to have an identity crisis. By the grace of God they — and they alone — are **GOD'S CHOSEN PEOPLE**.

THE SOVEREIGN GOD'S OVERVIEW
OF BOTH JEW AND GENTILE

Before we proceed further, two vital issues need to be addressed: man's human nature and the Sovereign God's overview of both Jew and Gentile. God is an equal opportunity truth teller. He "lays it on the line" right across the board — regarding all races and ethnic groups. His word clearly states that "**all** have sinned and come short of the glory of God" (*Romans* 3:23). Sin is our natural state — it's our "adoing what comes naturally." It's the everyday manifestation of who — **AND WHAT** — we are, of and by ourselves.

In our normal, natural, carnal (fleshly) state we automatically produce what the Bible terms "the works of the flesh" (*Galatians* 5:19). These works include adultery, fornication, idolatry, witchcraft, hatred, wrath, strife, seditions, envyings, murder, drunkenness, revellings, and such like (vs.19-22). In one form or another, participating in such activities is "as easy as falling off a log" for the average human being. It's called "sinning."

Naturally speaking, this is the way of the world, the way things actually are in real life — as well as in books, magazines, on TV and in the movies. This condition is part and parcel of our fallen nature. It's a "constant" undeniably reflected in the history of the human race since the Fall. It is the stuff of which history is made. We may use all types of sophistry ("fallacious reasoning; reasoning sound in appearance only", Webster) to deny this hideous genetically-inherited flaw in humankind, but the basic proof of its existence bombards us from every point of the compass.

Interestingly, while many in today's society are increasingly brazen and "in your face" with their wilful rebellion and criminal activity, most are incredibly ingenious in the camouflages they employ to cover up what is really happening in their miserable lives.

This undeniable reality proves the perfect accuracy with which God, in the Bible, portrays man's natural condition since the Fall: "God saw that the wickedness of man was great on the earth, and that every imagination of the thoughts of his heart was only evil continually" (*Genesis* 6:5). Man is naturally "abominable and filthy ... [He] drinks iniquity like water" (*Job* 15:16). "The heart of man **IS** deceitful above all things and **desperately wicked**, who can know it?" (*Jeremiah* 17:9). "The carnal mind [the natural, fleshy, carnal (meaty) mind with which we are all born] **IS** enmity against God: for **it is not subject to the law of God, neither indeed can be**" (*Romans* 8:7).

We need to acknowledge and understand that this fallen state — which results in the emptiness, anguish, and human frustration we see all around us — is universal in nature. **It blankets every individual of every nationality, race, or ethnic group— from the top to the bottom. There are no exceptions.** In biblical terms, they are all said to be "dead in trespasses and sins" (*Ephesians* 2:1). They will all, black, white, brown, yellow — Jew and Gentile alike — remain in that empty, helpless, despairing condition **unless** something totally **supernatural** — and altogether beyond their control — occurs in their lives.

No amount of spiritual mumbo-jumbo, or any amount of "avoidance behavior" and mental gymnastics can redeem them or be of any use in changing their natural condition. No amount of "self improvement" exercises, "self-realization" classes, "attitude adjustments," or "political correctness" will be of any consequence. These are all humanly-devised, phony forms of artificial resuscitation. They can, at best, improve the vain "self image" of those who participate in such activities. They are all clear manifestations of man's belief in the Satanic lie that he — mankind collectively — can "be as gods" (*Genesis* 3:5) and thus work out his own salvation without assistance.

YOU MUST BE BORN AGAIN

Most are oblivious of the fact that, to enjoy the truly abundant life, they must be "born again." To most, such a spiritual concept is unintelligible. It's beyond their comprehension. It draws a "blank" on their mental computer screens. Scripture says, "it is to them that perish foolishness; **but unto us which ARE saved it is the power of God**" (*I Corinthians* 1:18).

The act of regeneration — or being "born again" — is totally supernatural. People don't "decide" to be born again. If they did, it would be "salvation by works" — and totally unscriptural. On the contrary, as the apostle Paul wrote to Timothy, **God "hath saved us and called us** with a holy calling, **not** according to our works, but **according to his own purpose and grace,** which was **given us** in Christ Jesus **before the world began**" (*II Timothy* 1:9).

This fact of divine intervention — in which the Sovereign God reaches down from his throne of grace and calls whom he will out of the Babylonian cesspool of iniquity which exists on planet earth — is demonstrated almost endlessly in scripture: "For **by grace are you saved**, through faith; and that **not** of yourselves: **it is the gift of God**" (*Ephesians* 2:8). "You has **he** quickened [made alive] who were **dead** in trespasses and sins" (*Ephesians* 2:1). "The wages of sin is death, but the **gift** of God is eternal life through Jesus Christ our Lord" (*Romans* 6:23).

"For the promise is unto you, and to your children, and to all that are afar off, even **as many as the Lord our God shall call**" (Acts 2:39).

"Being confident of this very thing, that **he [God] which has begun a good work in you** will perform it until the day of our Lord Jesus Christ" (*Philippians* 1:6).

"He that **heareth** my word and **believeth** on him that sent me **HATH ETERNAL LIFE** and shall not come into condemnation, but **IS PASSED FROM DEATH UNTO LIFE**" (*John* 5:24). Notice from scripture that only Christ's "sheep" are capable of "hearing" and responding to his voice, or calling (*John* 10:27). Only they have "spiritual" antennas. Says Christ, "I **give** unto **them** eternal life; and **they** shall never perish, neither shall **any** man pluck them out of my hand. My father, **which gave them me,** is greater than all; and **no man** is able to pluck **them** out of my father's hand" (vs.28,29).

BROUGHT IMMORTALITY TO LIGHT THROUGH THE GOSPEL

Now, note another particularly important scripture. "**Jesus Christ ... hath abolished death and hath brought life and immortality to light through the gospel**" (*II Timothy* 1:10). The names of God's elect — Jew and Gentile alike — were "written in the book of life from the foundation of the world" (*Revelation* 17:8). As far as they — personally and individually — were concerned, that glorious fact was only brought to light when, by the grace of God, they were finally able to **"hear"** the good news (gospel) of their salvation. "[A]s **many as** were **ordained to eternal life** believed" (*Acts* 13:48).

Another critical verse: "**He that hears my word and believes HATH everlasting life ... and IS passed from death unto life**" (*John* 5:24). Notice that this preexisting state was **"brought to light"** through the gospel. Again, that is God's decision — not ours! "For **by grace are you saved**, through faith; and that **not** of yourselves; **it is the gift of God**" (*Ephesians* 2:8). Christ is our only hope of glory (*Colossians* 1:27). In the salvation process, the initiative **always** comes from God, never from man!

"For as the Father raiseth up the dead, and quickeneth them; **even so the Son quickeneth [makes alive] WHOM HE WILL**" (*John* 5:21). As Jesus said to the Pharisees, "**He that is of God heareth God's** words; ye therefore hear them NOT because ye are NOT of God" (*John* 8:47).

The Sovereign God causes HIS people to be born again BECAUSE they are his Chosen people!

A physical example may, to some small degree, serve to illustrate this amazing truth, this divine spiritual reality. When we were conceived by our earthly parents — purposely, accidentally, or otherwise — we were totally oblivious to the fact. When we were born, physically, we were consciously unaware of the miraculous event that had just taken place. A baby doesn't have anything to do with his conception or birth. He doesn't decide to be conceived ... or born. Both events are completely beyond his control. He doesn't finally realise that he's "here" until months after the event has actually taken place.

Likewise, when one is "born again" it is not the result of any action on the part of the individual involved. In their best state they are altogether vanity (*Psalm* 39:5). They are lost, blind, dead in their trespasses and sins (*Ephesians* 2:1) — far beyond "saving" themselves. When that miraculous event — that amazing divine intervention — takes place in their lives, they can truly echo the words of John Newton's immortal hymn, *Amazing Grace*:

> Amazing grace! how sweet the sound,
> That saved a wretch like me!
> I once was lost, but now am found, Was blind, but now I see.
>
> Twas grace that taught my heart to fear,
> And grace my fears relieved;
> How precious did that grace appear The hour I first believed.
>
> Thro' many dangers, toils, and snares,
> I have already come;
> 'Tis grace hath bro't me safe thus far, And grace will lead me home.
>
> When we've been there ten thousand years,
> Bright shining as the sun,
> We've no less days to sing God's praise Than when we'd first begun.

A SIMPLE BUT PROFOUND TRUTH

Most may have overlooked a simple but profound truth. Why did the Creator choose to use the term "born again"? Upon reflection, the answer seems obvious. The analogy or symbolism of human birth was chosen to express the utter impossibility of a spiritual "birth" taking place spontaneously — without the help of a father. **The rebirth is spiritual in nature. The law of biogenesis dictates that spiritual life can only come from preexisting life of the same kind.** As God is spirit (*John* 4:24) and man is flesh, it is obvious that spiritual life can only emanate from God. As scripture says, "that which is born of the flesh IS flesh, and that which is born of the spirit IS spirit" (*John* 3:6).

Jesus' disciples enquired, "Who ... can be saved?" His reply: **"With men this is impossible, but with God all things are possible"** (*Matthew* 19:24,26).

Please notice the word "see" in *John* 3:3: "Except a man be born again, he cannot **SEE** the kingdom of God." That "seeing" is spiritual in character, and revolutionizes every aspect of their existence. Those who are spiritually "blind" and "deaf" are unable to see and hear what the born again Christian can see and hear. "For the kingdom of God is **not** meat and drink [physical in nature], but **righteousness and peace in the Holy Spirit**" (*Romans* 14:17).

This is the faith which was **"once delivered to the saints"** (*Jude* 1:3). The faith whereby **"all things ... become new"** (*II Corinthians* 5:17). This is the glorious truth that "turned the world upside down" in the first century (*Acts* 17:6). The spiritual transformation takes place in the lives of the elect as a result of, **under the new covenant,** God placing his law in their inward parts and writing it in their hearts. He becomes their God, and they become his people (*Jeremiah* 31:31). This is a sovereign act of God.

As the redeemed of God, they become **new creations in Christ** (*Galatians* 6:15). **"In Christ Jesus, ye who sometimes were far off are made nigh by the blood of Christ.**

"For he **is** our peace.... [Through him we] are builded together as a habitation of God through the spirit" (*Ephesians* 2:13,14,22). "Know ye not that **ye are the temple of God**, and that the Spirit of God dwelleth in **you**?" (*I Corinthians* 3:16). In Christ, the elect "are a chosen generation, a royal priesthood, a peculiar people; that we should show forth the praises of him that called us **out of** darkness **into** his most marvelous light" (*I Peter* 2:9). "Therefore **if** any man be **in Christ, he is a new creature**; old things are passed away, **all things are become new**" (*II Corinthians* 5:17). **As God's children, they are "heirs of God, and joint heirs with Christ** ... that we may be also glorified together" (*Romans* 8:17).

They are working out their own salvation in fear and trembling **FOR** it is **God** who works in them to **WILL** and to **DO** of **HIS** good pleasure (*Philippians* 2:13). On the cross Christ paid the penalty for their sins and made them his own. **"There is therefore no condemnation to those who are in Christ Jesus"** (*Romans* 8:1). In their lives they are bearing the fruit of the Holy Spirit — love, joy, peace, long-suffering, gentleness, goodness, faith, **"against which there is no law"** (*Galatians* 5:22-23). Christ **IS** their life (*Colossians* 1:27). As such, they are "blessed with all spiritual blessings in heavenly places in Christ" (*Ephesians* 1:3).

They know the truth and the truth has made them free (*John* 8:32). "If the Son therefore shall make you free you shall be free indeed" (*John* 8:36). Indeed means "in reality, in truth, in fact" (*Webster*).

GOD'S CHOSEN PEOPLE — THE "ISRAEL OF GOD"

In this booklet, the reader has been bombarded with — one could say almost marinated in — literally hundreds of "thus saith the Lord" verses. These prove beyond a shadow of doubt that God's elect are redeemed and saved through the death, resurrection, and ascension of our Lord Jesus Christ. They are God's Chosen People — the "Israel of God." The author has never attempted, even remotely, to impose his own belief system on his readers. Recognizing the biblical fact that no scripture is of private interpretation (*II Peter* 1:20), he has, page after page, faithfully quoted chapter and verse — **thus letting God's word interpret itself.** "[L]et God be true and every man a liar" (*Romans* 3:4).

MOST DON'T WANT TO BE CONFUSED WITH THE FACTS

Considerable experience indicates, however, that most don't want to be confused with biblical facts. In most cases, their minds have been soaked in denominational dogma from youth. **"After their own lusts, they heap to themselves false teachers, having itching ears, and they turn away their ears from the truth and are turned unto fables"** (*II*

Timothy 4:3-4). Through radio and television, they have been heavily influenced by a variety of glib, fast-talking religion con artists and shysters. They have been made to "feel good." Unfortunately, such religious slop also makes them fat, lazy, and sick — spiritually speaking. They are actually dying of spiritual malnutrition.

To paraphrase lawyer Gerry Spence, their minds are packed to the ceiling with religious junk so that nothing of true value can get in. When the door opens they, like parrots in a pet shop, spew out mindless, frequently conflicting mantras. They have no concept of sound doctrine. Confusion reigns.

There is no thinking taking place. Growth is dead. Learning is gridlocked. They won't endure sound doctrine. You can drown such prejudiced people in biblical truths, in documented facts, in reason and in logic, but your efforts will usually go for naught. You had just as well sing to a bag of jelly beans.

When confronted with biblical reality, such as that regarding the true identity of God's Chosen People and the doctrine of election, they perceive it to be an attack on them, personally. Or on their belief system — regardless of its lack of veracity. They rarely adopt the biblical position of, "Come, let us reason together" (*Isaiah* 1:18).

In their biblical illiteracy, their minds automatically shift into a defensive mode. They frequently resort to name-calling, a tactic employed by the Florida-based evangelist mentioned at the beginning of this booklet. Pathetic! Absent that, they start quoting such perceived Bible "authorities" as Cyrus Scofield, Hal Lindsey, John Hagee, Jerry Falwell, or whatever new "prophet," evangelist, or "man of God" happens to be skipping through town and has their fleeting attention at that moment.

"**They can't ALL be wrong, CAN THEY?**" In their distorted theological overview, clear, indisputable Bible verses become "just your opinion."

Would to God that **HIS** word was engraved on their consciousness instead of the error they now embrace.

A BLATANT MISAPPLICATION OF GOD'S WORD

Unable to refute biblical truth, they start throwing out Bible verses which, when taken in context, serve only to prove the fallacy of their own position. In their spiritual stupor, they are unable to grasp the fact that a text taken out of context is a pretext.

One such scripture is found in *Romans* 11. In verse 26 of that chapter, they read the words "all Israel shall be saved." Not understanding the difference between spiritual "Israel" that exists within physical "Israel," to them, this "proves" that all physical Israelites who have ever lived will be saved and will lead the world into an unprecedented period of peace and prosperity in what they term the Millennium. The huge difference between these two groups (light as opposed to darkness) is underlined in *Romans* 9:27-29. These verses eliminate any idea of there being an unqualified "Israel." Had not God saved a remnant, they would personally be suffering the same fate as Sodom and Gomorrah. According to Jude 7, these two cities "**are set forth for an example, suffering [present tense] the vengeance of eternal fire.**" The prophet Isaiah indicates that the remnant saved out of physical Israel consists of a tenth (*Isaiah* 6:13).

The blatant misapplication of God's word by most Millennialists only goes to prove two things: their abysmal ignorance of scripture and their unwillingness to do as did the first-century Bereans (*Acts* 17:11). Of all the books in the Bible, Paul's letter to the saints at Rome (*Romans* 1:6-7) — probably more than any other — documents the identity of the "Israel of God," referred to in *Galatians* 6. Scripture clearly proves that this elect group is exclusively made up of the children of promise. Paul declares: "**Now we, brethren, AS ISAAC WAS, are the children of promise**" (*Galatians* 4:28). On the day of Pentecost, Peter stated that "**the promise is to ... AS MANY AS the Lord our God shall call**" (*Acts* 2:39). Paul nails it down further: "They which **ARE** the children of the flesh, these are **NOT** the children of God: **BUT the children of the promise ARE counted AS the seed**"(*Romans* 9:8). Could anything be clearer? Hardly!

ISAAC AND THE CHILDREN OF PROMISE

Notice carefully this reference to Isaac. It's vitally important. The story behind Isaac's birth serves to explain the true meaning of "the promise." In scripture, "the promise" — as shown earlier — begins in the book of *Genesis*. In chapter eleven, we come across the first mention of Abram (later Abraham). Aged 75, Abram lived in Ur of the

Chaldees with his wife Sarai (later Sarah). Sarai "was barren; she had no children" (*Genesis* 11:30).

The society in which they lived was morally depraved. It was little if any better than the pre-Flood world that preceded it. Of that world it was written that "God saw that the wickedness of man ... was great and that every imagination of his heart was only evil continually" (*Genesis* 6:5). Of the post-Flood period it was written that there was none that did good, no not one (*Romans* 3:10,12). That included Abram. He was dead in his trespasses and sins — oblivious to spiritual reality. Abram would have remained in that sordid condition were it not for the fact that the Creator God revealed himself to him as the Sovereign of the universe.

The Lord revealed himself to Abram. Abram didn't volunteer for service. God told him to, "**get out** of thy country, and **from** thy kindred, and **from** thy father's house, unto a land that I shall shew you.

"**And I will make of thee a great nation, and I will bless thee, and thou shalt be a blessing.**

"**And I will bless them that bless thee, and curse him that curses thee, and in thee shall all nations of the earth be blessed**" (*Genesis* 12:1-3). Notice that it was God who thought up and laid out each phase of this long-term plan. **None of this was Abram's idea.** In faith [**faith is a gift of God, and a fruit of the Holy Spirit** (*Galatians* 5:22)], Abram obeyed God. He left the pagan, moon-worshipping environment into which he had been born, and in which he had previously felt at home. This was "counted to him for righteousness" (*Genesis* 15:6).

But there was an ongoing problem. God had **PROMISED** Abram that in his seed all nations of the earth would be blessed. Twenty-five years went by, and no heir emerged. Humanly speaking, it appeared as if God may have broken his promise to Abram.

Then, God appeared once more to Abram, declaring himself to be his "shield and exceeding great reward" (15:1). Abram complained that, "I go childless ... thou hast given me no seed" (v.2). As a result, Abram thought he might have to make one of the children born to one of his concubines (a bondwoman) his heir. God said no. "This shall **not** be your heir; **but** he that shall come forth **out of thy own bowels shall be thine heir**" (v.4). He further told Abram: "Look now toward heaven, and tell the stars. If thou be able to number them, so shall thy seed be" (v.5).

As more time passed, Sarai — Abram's wife — became increasingly impatient. She allowed her fertile mind to work overtime. Why not, she thought, give her Egyptian handmaiden (Hagar) to her husband "that I might obtain children by her" (*Genesis* 16:2). In a moment of weakness, this human solution appealed to Abram, "and he hearkened to the voice of Sarai" (v.2). Abram was 86 years old when Hagar bare Ishmael to Abram (16:16). This was one of those things that "looked good" and "seemed right" at the time, but which later resulted in long-term strife. The son born to the bondwoman was named Ishmael.

Still more time passed. Abram was 99. Sarai was 90. Abram was impotent. Sarai was barren. Both were past the age when it was **HUMANLY** possible to have children. Yet **"THE PROMISE"** made by God to Abram was still unfulfilled.

It was at this crucial juncture — when all **human** hope of an heir had vanished — that God appeared once again to Abram, **changing his name to Abraham.** He reminded Abraham of **the promise** he had made many years before. Regarding Sarai, whose name was now changed to Sarah, God said: "I will bless her and she shall be the mother of nations; kings of people shall be of her" (*Genesis* 17:15,16). To both Abraham and Sarah this still seemed impossible. Abraham asked: "Shall a child be born to him that is an hundred years old, and shall Sarah that is ninety years old, bear?" He was still thinking of Ishmael being his heir (vs.17,18).

God replied: "Sarah thy wife **shall** bear thee a son indeed [in reality, in truth] and **thou shalt call his name Isaac; and I shall establish my covenant with him for an everlasting covenant, and with his seed after him"** (v.19).

Later, "Sarah conceived and bare Abraham a son in his old age, at the set time at which God had spoken to him. And Abraham called the name of his son ... Isaac" (*Genesis* 21:2-3). Abraham now had his **promised** son. From Isaac would come Jacob (later Israel), from whose progeny would eventually come Jesus Christ the Messiah. In him and through him would all the nations of the earth be blessed. **NOTICE VERY CAREFULLY THAT GOD FULFILLS HIS PROMISES WHEN IT IS TOTALLY IMPOSSIBLE FOR MAN TO DO ANYTHING ON HIS OWN.** "With men it is impossible, but not with God; for with God all things are possible" (*Mark* 10:27). When we grasp that one simple but very powerful fact we begin to understand

God's new covenant and overall plan for mankind. It perfectly explains what Paul wrote: "To Abraham and his seed [singular] were the promises made. He saith **NOT**, And to seeds [plural] as of many; but as of one, And to thy seed which is Christ."

"And **IF** ye be Christ's, **THEN** are ye Abraham's seed **AND HEIRS ACCORDING TO THE PROMISE**" (*Galatians* 3:16,29). Born again Christians — those whom God has called and whose lives have been changed from the inside out — are clearly "the children of promise." They are "a chosen generation, a royal priesthood, a holy nation, a peculiar people [so that they] should show forth the praises of him that called [them] out of darkness [like he did Abraham] into his most marvelous light:

"**Which in time past were not a people, BUT ARE NOW THE [SINGULAR] PEOPLE OF GOD**" (*I Peter* 2:9,10).

IDENTIFYING "THE CHILDREN OF PROMISE"

With these irrefutable **biblical facts** securely in mind, let us now examine one of the most critically important sections of the New Testament — *Romans*, chapters nine through eleven. Understanding the identity of the children of promise, the elect, the remnant, and the Israel of God, is the key that unlocks this otherwise hard to understand portion of God's word.

In *Romans* **9, the Apostle Paul is unquestionably speaking about two different "Israels."** Who are these? In *Galatians* 6:16, Paul speaks of the "Israel of God." Obviously, by the power of logical deduction, if there is an "Israel of God" there must — of necessity — be **another** "Israel," one that is **not** of God.

The reader will remember from earlier in this booklet that the Lord Jesus Christ condemned the leaders of physical Israel in no uncertain terms. He said that they, having rejected the true God, were "**of [their] father the devil**" (*John* 8:44). He declared that they were "**full of hypocrisy and iniquity**" and were "**serpents and a generation of vipers.**" Upon them would "come all the righteous blood shed upon the earth, from the blood of righteous Abel unto the blood of Zacharias... **Verily [truly] I say unto you, ALL these things SHALL come upon THIS generation... Behold your house IS left unto you desolate**" (*Matthew* 23:28,33,35,36,38). "**Therefore say I unto you, The** kingdom of God shall be taken from you, and given to a nation bringing forth the fruits thereof"** (*Matthew* 21: 43).

God's covenant with **physical** Israel was thus finally terminated in 70 AD. From then on, he was to deal exclusively with the new, spiritual Israel — the "Israel of God" — those who are now "the people of God." This glorious fact is nailed down in *Romans* 2:28,29.

ROMANS CHAPTER NINE

Paul opens this chapter with the declaration that he is telling "the truth in Christ **[in whom the promise was fulfilled]**, I lie not, my conscience bearing me witness in the Holy Spirit." He had "great heaviness and continual sorrow" in his heart.

"For I **COULD** [if he had not understood that "truth in Christ"] wish that myself were accursed from Christ **for my brethren, MY KINSMEN ACCORDING TO THE FLESH** [physical Israel]" (vs.1,2)

Paul then goes on to explain the truth about the two "Israels." "They are **not** all [spiritual] Israel which are of [physical] Israel.

"**Neither** because they **are** the seed of Abraham, are they all children [of promise]: **but, in Isaac shall thy seed by called.**

"**That is, They which are the children of the flesh [physical Israel], these are NOT the children of God, BUT the children of the promise ARE counted for the seed.**

"For **THIS IS THE WORD OF PROMISE**, at this time will I come, and Sarah shall have a son.

"And not only this; But when Rebecca also had conceived by one, even by our father Isaac;

"**For** the children [of Rebecca] being **not yet born, NEITHER HAVING DONE ANY GOOD OR EVIL**, that the purpose of God **ACCORDING TO ELECTION** might stand, **NOT** of works [anything man can do] **but of him that calleth** ..." (*Romans* 9:6-11). Only "**the children of the promise ARE counted for the seed.**" Again, let God be true, and every man a liar!

"THE PEOPLE WHICH HE FOREKNEW"

But how about the "other Israel" — as Paul says, Israel "of the flesh"? Paul deals specifically with this question in the middle of *Romans* 11.

But first he deals with the Israel of promise. "I say then, has God cast away **HIS** people? God forbid.... God has **NOT** cast away **HIS PEOPLE WHICH HE FOREKNEW**" (vs.1,2). Now what about the "other Israel" — they that killed God's prophets, digged down his altars, and sought Paul's life (v.3)?

"But what sayeth the answer of God...? I have reserved to myself seven thousand men [a symbolic number of completion], who have **not** bowed the knee to the image of Baal.

"Even so at this present time also there is **a remnant according to the election of grace**.

"And if by grace [spiritual Israel], then it is no more of works; otherwise grace is no more grace. But if it be of works [physical Israel], then it is no more grace; otherwise work is no more work" (vs.4-6).

"**What then?** Israel [physical] has **NOT** obtained that which he seeketh for, **BUT THE ELECTION [SPIRITUAL ISRAEL, THE CHILDREN OF PROMISE] HATH OBTAINED IT, and the rest were blinded.**

"(According as it is written, **God HATH given them the spirit of slumber, eyes that they should NOT see, and ears that they should NOT hear;) unto this day.**

"And David saith, **Let** their table be made a snare, and a trap, and a stumbling block, and a recompense unto them.

"**Let** their eyes be darkened **that** they may **not** see, and their ears that they should **not** hear, and **bow down their back alway**" (vs.7-10). "Alway" (or always) is defined as: "**Permanently, throughout all time, as, God is always the same**" (Webster).

In other words, it's "all over" for physical Israel. All the prophecies of the Old Testament have been vindicated. Physical Israel "sowed the wind and reaped the whirlwind." They are now "history."

In the remaining verses of chapter eleven, Paul shows that a number of physical Israelites — elect and nonelect alike — will continue to live side by side "until the fulness of the Gentiles be come in" (v. 25). At that time, or at the coming of Christ, the remaining elect will be called. **They will be grafted into the olive tree, representing the Israel of God. Thus "all Israel shall be saved..." (v.26). Truly, "The gifts and calling of God are without repentance" (v.29).**

To those who believe this is unfair, and who may be very upset with the biblically-documented state of affairs, God replies: "**O man, Who** art thou that repliest against God. Shall the thing formed say to him that formed it, Why hast thou made me thus?" (*Romans* 9:20).

Once again, Let God be true and every man a liar.

"GOD ... HAS PREPARED FOR THEM A CITY"

One very important question remains to be answered from the pages of God's word: What is the ultimate reward "hoped for" by both physical Israel and spiritual Israel, "the [singular] Israel of God" (*Galatians* 6:16)?

In *Acts* 25 we read that "the high priest and the chief of the Jews" in Jerusalem developed an elaborate plot to get rid of the apostle Paul. They informed the Roman authorities against him and demanded that they send Paul, who was imprisoned in Caesarea, to Jerusalem to stand trial. They planned to ambush him along the way and kill him (vs.1-3).

The Jewish leaders sent their agents to Caesarea. There, they laid "many and grievous complaints against Paul, which they could not prove" (v.7). Sensing that his life was in imminent danger, Paul appealed to Caesar (vs.10-11). As a result, he was taken to the capital of the Roman Empire.

In Rome, Paul "called the chief of the Jews together." His purpose? "I called for you, to see you, and to speak to you, **BECAUSE THAT FOR THE HOPE OF ISRAEL I AM BOUND WITH THIS CHAIN**" (*Acts* 28:20).

It is obvious that "the hope of Israel" envisioned by Paul clashed with that embraced by the Jewish leaders of the first century. Their conflicting worldviews lay at the heart of the Pharisees' vicious antagonism toward their former compatriot. In their spiritual stupor, they saw Paul as "a pestilent fellow and a mover of sedition among the Jews throughout the world, and a ringleader of the sect of the Nazarenes" (*Acts* 24:5). They wanted him killed. Remember that prior to his miraculous conversion on the road to Damascus Paul had belonged to "the most straitest sect of our [Jewish] religion." He was a Pharisee (*Acts* 26:5).

Paul declared that he was being "judged for the hope of the promise made of God unto our fathers." As we proved earlier from scripture, that **promise** was centered on and fulfilled in our Lord Jesus Christ. **It** was for this "hope's sake [that he was] accused of the Jews"** (vs.6,7).

It is clear that from the beginning the gospel preached by Paul was focused on the sovereignty of God, the inerrancy of scripture, and the Lordship of Jesus Christ. The resurrection of the dead was a vital part of his message: "[O]f the hope of the resurrection I am called in question" (*Acts* 23:6). "[T]here shall be a resurrection of the dead, both of the just and the unjust... Touching the resurrection of the dead I am called in question by you this day" (*Acts* 24:15,21). "Why should it be thought a thing incredible with you, that God should raise the dead?" (*Acts* 26:8). Christ's resurrection was at the core of the gospel preached by the apostles (*Acts* 1:22; 2:24,31,32; 3:15,26; 4:2,10; 4:33).

ANOTHER "HOPE"

Physical Israel, which rejected Jesus the Messiah with such venom, had another "hope." They had visions of a physical kingdom — one completely under their control — ruling the nations of the world with a rod of iron. Modern "Jews" — who are mostly non-Hebrew, non-Semitic Khazars with no lawful, biblical claim to Palestine — cling doggedly to the same false "hope."

In a short article in *Look magazine* (January 16, 1962, p.20), then Israeli Prime Minister David Ben Gurion laid out his "image of the world" that lay ahead. The United States would be turned into "a welfare state with a planned economy" on the way to creating a world government. "All armies will be abolished, and there will be no more wars. **In Jerusalem**, the United Nations (a truly *United* Nations) will build a Shrine to the Prophets to serve the federated union of all continents; **this will be the seat of the Supreme Court of Mankind, to settle all controversies among the federated continents, as prophesied by Isaiah.**"

This basic theme is popular in Jewish writings. For example, Rabbi Michael Higger wrote what amounts to a compendium of Rabbinism's views on the "ideal" social order planned for your future. He labels it "the Kingdom of God."

The learned rabbi asks: "How will this ideal civilization take root?... A model, ideal state comprising a group of righteous individuals and living an ideal life, will gradually spread its teachings and influence from nation to nation, throughout the world. **The Kingdom of God will then become a fact.**

"Israel is the only nation united to that purpose...

"The people of Israel will thus conquer, **SPIRITUALLY**, the nations of the earth, so that Israel will be made high above all nations in praise, in name, and in glory" (*The Jewish Utopia*, pgs. 29-30).

"Conquer, **SPIRITUALLY**"? That could only be accomplished through spiritual seduction.

Rabbi Roland B. Gittlesohn: "What do Jews believe about the Messiah?... [T]hey do not expect the Messiah to be the Son of God. Most non-Orthodox Jews hinge their hopes more on a messianic age than on an individual messiah." Rabbi Gittlesohn then quotes an unnamed rabbi: "There is a spark of messiah in all of us; when we [Jews] succeed in putting together all our individual sparks, the result will constitute the coming of the messiah" (*The Meaning of Judaism*, World Publishing Company, 1956, pp. 50-51).

Dr. Arthur Klausner elaborates: "Thus the whole people Israel [i.e. the Jews or Talmudists] in the form of the elect of the nation gradually become the Messiah of the world, the Redeemer of mankind" (*The Messianic Idea of Israel*, Bradford and Dickens, 1956, p.163).

Who, you may ask, will own everything if this Jewish "Messianic" vision comes to fruition? Jewish author Samuel Roth provides the answer: "The Jews pride themselves on their reluctance to proselytize. They explain that this is a sign not only of their religious exclusiveness, but of their good will towards the rest of the religions. **It is nothing of the sort. The Jews do not proselytize because they are firmly convinced that they will eventually inherit the earth, and they want as few claimants as possible to this windfall**" (*Jews Must Live*, 1934, p.28).

"IF YOU WILL FALL DOWN AND WORSHIP ME"

Whose fabulous idea was it to create a physical "kingdom of heaven" on earth with Jesus Christ as king? The answer will surprise many.

In *Matthew* chapter 4, we read that "Jesus was led up of the Spirit into the wilderness **to be tempted of the devil.**

"And when he had fasted forty days and forty nights ... the devil takes him up into an exceeding high mountain." There, Satan conjured up a glowing picture of the fabulous physical kingdom that he (Satan) would give Christ IF he would go along with his agenda. Satan laid

before Christ "**all** the kingdoms of the world, and the **glory** of them."
It was an offer of unparalleled earthly power, honor and prestige.

"**ALL** these things will I give you, **IF YOU WILL FALL DOWN AND WORSHIP ME**"(*Matthew* 4:8-9).

What was the Savior's response to Satan's dazzling proposition? How did he look upon the idea of establishing at Jerusalem a "kingdom of heaven" ruling over "**all** the kingdoms of the world"?

"**Get thee hence, Satan: for it is written, You shall worship the Lord your God, and him only shall you serve**" (v.10).

Now, notice carefully: "From **THAT** time [his initial conquest of Satan] Jesus **BEGAN** to preach, and to say, **THE KINGDOM OF HEAVEN IS AT HAND** (4:17). In others words, the true kingdom of heaven [not a Satanic counterfeit] was about to commence right then in the first century. It was a very different type of kingdom than that proposed by Satan. It was **spiritual** in nature.

"For the kingdom of God is **NOT** meat and drink [physical in nature], **but righteousness, and peace, in the Holy Spirit**" (*Romans* 14:17). "[T]he hour comes, **AND NOW IS,** when the true worshipers shall worship the Father **in spirit and in truth**: for the Father seeks **such** to worship him.

"God is Spirit, and they that worship him **must** worship him in spirit and in truth" (*John* 4:23-24).

This is in perfect harmony with the New Covenant sealed by the blood of the Lord Jesus Christ (*Matthew 26:28* and *Mark* 14:24). **Under this blood covenant, God puts his law in our inward parts and writes it in our hearts. We thus become his people, and he becomes our God** (*Jeremiah* 31:31-34). We have been "bought with a price" and are no longer the "servants of men" (*I Corinthians* 7:23). We become "new creature[s]; old things are passed away; behold, all things are become new" (*II Corinthians* 5:17). Unlike those around us, we have "another king, one Jesus" (*Acts* 17:7).

Such a miraculous transformation can't come about as a result of our own physical or mental efforts — anything we can do, personally: "With men it is **impossible**, but **not** with God; for with God all things are possible" (*Mark* 10:27). **It is God who puts his law in our inward parts and writes it in our hearts.**

A STRONG DELUSION

Untold millions of naive, biblically illiterate "Christians" have given heed to Jewish fables regarding a coming global utopia headquartered in Jerusalem. They have turned away from biblical truth (*Titus* 1:14; *II Timothy* 4:4). Because they are much more "excited" by fantasy than by biblical revelation, God has sent them strong delusion that they should believe a lie (*II Thessalonians* 2:11). Although their Bibles clearly reveal that today's Jerusalem is **"the great city, which SPIRITUALLY is called Sodom and Egypt, where also our Lord was crucified"** (*Revelation* 11:8), most Bible "students" read over that fact as if it didn't exist. The spiritual truth revealed in this vital scripture is deeply buried under the spiritual garbage that has accumulated in the non-thinking, non-perceptive minds of untold millions of otherwise honest and sincere people. They have been spiritually seduced by damnable heresies masquerading under such labels as "Judeo-Christianity" and "Christian-Zionism." Having no basis in scripture, this endtime apostasy has devastated the Christian community.

Professor Daniel Boyarin — a Talmudic student at Berkeley — reveals that, **"The term 'Judeo-Christian' was invented in the 1930s**... It was originally ... developed as an anti-Fascist **TOOL**, against** people who wanted to insist that America is a Christian culture and that Jews don't belong here. **So liberal Christians, together with Jews, produced the NOTION of a common heritage called the Judeo-Christian tradition**, to incorporate Jews into the American socius" (*The California Monthly,* an Alumni Association organ at the University of California at Berkeley. February 2000). Note well: The utterly fantastic **NOTION** of 'Judeo-Christianity' is the product of non-Bible-believing "liberal Christians" in league with Talmudic Jews who despise our Lord Jesus Christ. The latter, like their first century counterparts, are "of [their] father the devil" (*John* 8:44). In furthering their plans to create a counterfeit "kingdom of heaven" on earth, the Judeo-Christian **"TOOL"** has proven invaluable.

"JERUSALEM ... MOTHER OF US ALL"

A physical "kingdom of heaven" headquartered in Jerusalem is **NOT** the hope of "the Israel of God" (*Galatians* 6:16). In his letter to his Christian brethren in Galatia, the apostle Paul expounded on the real hope of the true Israel: that embodied in **"THE PROMISE."** He rejected the false "hope" embraced by physical Israel, stating that "Jerusalem which **now** is ... **is IN BONDAGE with her children.**

"But Jerusalem which is above is FREE ... is the mother of us all" (*Galatians* 4:23,25,26). In the book of *Hebrews*, Paul elaborates: "But **YOU** are come [present tense] unto ... **the city of the living God, the heavenly Jerusalem,** and to an innumerable company of angels" (*Hebrews* 12:22). The hope of the Christian is **not** a strip of sand along the coast of the Mediterranean Sea, **but rather the New Jerusalem which is above.**

Bearing in mind the "promise," we are also assured that Abraham (and others of like faith) embraced the same hope, "for he looked for a city which has foundations, whose builder and maker is God" (*Hebrews* 11:10). Like Abraham, "these all died in faith, not having received the promises, but having seen them afar off, and were persuaded of them, and embraced them, and confessed that **they were strangers and pilgrims on the earth...**

"But now **they desire a better country, that is, an heavenly**: wherefore God is not ashamed to be called their God: **for he has prepared for them a city [Heavenly Jerusalem]**" (*Hebrews* 11:13,16).

THAT IS THE TRUE HOPE OF GOD'S CHOSEN PEOPLE, THE ISRAEL OF GOD!

APPENDIX I

What Do You Mean, Truth?

By Des Griffin

What do you think about ...? Why do you believe ...? Have your ever considered ...? Why don't you give me just the facts? These and similar questions have fallen on hard times in the United States of the early part of the twenty-first century. In fact, one can get into serious trouble — and be socially ostracized — for having the audacity to ask questions of a serious nature regarding things that pertain to the future well-being of our once great nation.

Although our modern society prides itself on its awesome achievements and ultra-sophistication, we are undoubtedly among the most shallow, most manipulated, most brainwashed — and least knowledgeable and understanding — people who have ever used the appellation, "civilized."

Through modern technology, we have access to more information from more sources than any other generation in history. On the World Wide Web, it's all at our fingertips. Yet — ignoring reality — we appear mindlessly dedicated to the relentless pursuit of those things that have undermined and ultimately destroyed all civilizations that have gone before.

Like the Romans of yesteryear, the American people are so absorbed in irrelevant trivia "that they [appear to have] lost all thought and care for real life." Most are caught up in a "feverish rush for excitement, for something new to feed the sated senses," (Jerome Carcopino, *Daily Life in Ancient Rome*).

Buried in our make-believe worlds of fantasy, self-deception, and escapism, we — individually and collectively — appear braindead. Have we in fact become incapable of asking candid, in-depth questions about — and of demanding honest answers to — the truly important issues in life? When, perchance, we stumble across someone who has the courage to address the true concerns of life head-on, do we usually jump up, brush ourselves off, and hurry on about our meaningless lives as if nothing had happened? Or, instead of making honest enquiry into the facts of a matter, do we immediately attack anyone who appears to make even the mildest attempt to "intrude" on our fantasy-worlds. As Samuel Coleridge observed some 200 years ago, "Experience informs us that the first defense of weak minds is to recriminate."

How we respond to perceived "challenges" speaks volumes about our honesty — or lack thereof. About our education — or lack thereof! Most have an almost impossible task recognizing that truth is truth! That facts are facts! That reality is reality! And that to believe and act otherwise is to court disaster. We can't assign reality to George Orwell's infamous "memory hole" without ultimately paying a hideous price.

Intellectual ability has little bearing on many of the decisions we make. The numerous almost unbelievable technological advances our nation has enjoyed in recent decades demonstrate how brilliantly innovative many Americans are. Philosophically speaking, however, our basic problem lies in the fact that most of us have, unwittingly, been programmed to accept as true numerous basic premises that are diametrically opposed to reality. From time immemorial, people with an agenda have been rewriting our figurative 3 x 5 cards. Their purpose is to direct and control the decisions we make in our daily lives.

GARBAGE IN, GARBAGE OUT!

It must be recognized that the decisions we make are only as good as the information, philosophy, or worldview upon which they are based. Garbage in, garbage out! When one begins with a false premise, one automatically ends up with a false conclusion. This principle applies to every area of human activity.

From youth, most people haven't been taught to think critically, analytically, logically, and lawfully. They emerge from their formal educational experience with a lot of knowledge (mostly trivia), but little or no understanding of what life itself is all about. Like sponges, they absorb a vast amount of fragmented material. Most of this is worthless junk that floats around their minds cluttering up their mental processes. They have never been taught to critically examine and analyze the information they absorb. They have neither proved or disproved it.

Through a lack of knowledge and understanding of basic reality, they have never developed an indepth worldview that can be successfully applied in their everyday lives. Most are left groping in

the dark. Life remains a murky mystery. They have been taught to earn a living, but not how to really live.

REFUSING TO DEAL WITH REALITY

Many classic examples of such spiritual insanity are found in scripture: In the book of *Acts*, for example, we read of the powerful Christian witness given by Stephen, a "man full of faith and of the Holy Spirit" (6:5). The results were phenomenal: "[T]he word of God increased; and the number of the disciples multiplied in Jerusalem greatly, and a great company of the priests were obedient to the faith" (v.7).

How did the Jewish religious leaders react when, after "disputing with Stephen ... [they] were not able to resist the wisdom and the spirit by which he spoke"? (v.9-10). **They accused him of blasphemy, "stirred up the people and the elders," and set up false witnesses in an effort to destroy him** (vs.12-13). Later, when that tactic misfired — and Stephen continued to speak out boldly — **"they were cut to the heart, and they gnashed on him with their teeth.... Then they cried out with a loud voice, and stopped their ears, and ran upon him with one accord. And they cast him out of the city, and stoned him"** (7:54, 57,58).

The hearts of these "blind leaders of the blind" (*Matthew* 15:14) were oblivious to spiritual reality. Though they took immense pride in their "righteousness" and religious zeal, their darkened minds were packed to the ceiling with religious junk — with spurious doctrines and distorted theology. These blinded them to spiritual reality. They just weren't equipped — psychologically or spiritually — to handle the truth about themselves and the society in which they lived. Their murderous reaction was triggered by the fact that the exposure of myths and biases can be so psychologically disruptive as to be tantamount to complete ego destruction.

Murder in blind rage is frequently the result. Though most such situations thankfully end before the actual taking of human life, murderous thoughts are almost always part of the equation. Remember, "the heart of man IS deceitful above all thing and desperately wicked" (*Jeremiah* 17:9). Murder (or murderous thoughts) come naturally to unregenerate man. It's one of the "works of the flesh" (*Galatians*

5:19,21). It is imperative that we recognize that human nature never changes. **It's a constant — except as a result of divine intervention!**

"GREAT IS DIANA OF THE EPHESIANS"

A somewhat similar scenario unfolded in a Gentile community also in the first century. In the book of *Acts*, we read that Paul's preaching of the Gospel literally turned the Roman world "upside down" (17.6). Actually, the Roman world was already upside down, spiritually speaking. The people worshipped a pantheon of pagan gods of their own choosing. The explosive impact of the Gospel ("the way of the Lord," or "that way" (18:25;19:9) was instrumental in revolutionizing tens of thousands of lives. Lives were being straightened out — set right side up! As a result, "there arose no small stir about that way" (19:23). After all, why not? Mass conversions spelled potential economic disaster for those religious racketeers who were growing wealthy by scamming the public. Their future financial well-being was on the line!

Demetrius, a silversmith, led the charge against spiritual reality. Calling together his fellow religious con artists, Demetrius reminded them of the source of their wealth. Then he sounded the alarm. "Not only in Ephesus, but almost throughout all Asia, **this Paul has persuaded and turned away much people, saying that they be no gods, which are made with hands.... [T]his our craft is in danger of being set at nought.**" If we don't act quickly and decisively "the temple of the great goddess Diana [will] be despised, and her magnificence [will] be destroyed, whom all Asia and the world worships" (*Acts* 19:24-27).

How did the fine, upstanding, highly respected leaders of the business community in Ephesus respond to this emotional appeal? Did they think long-term by addressing their dilemma in an honest, rational manner? Did they demand to be apprised of all the relevant facts? Did they carefully consider all the pros and cons regarding the long-term welfare of the society in which they lived? Did they rejoice in the miraculous changes taking place in society — or were they mainly concerned with their own immediate financial interests?

Scripture reveals that, in their spiritual blindness, they voted with their wallets, for strictly short-term financial gain: "**[T]hey were full** of wrath, and cried out, saying, 'Great is Diana of the Ephesians.'" As a result, "the whole city was full of confusion.... Some therefore cried one thing, and some another; for the assembly was confused; and the more part knew not wherefore they were come together" (*Acts* 19:28,29,32). Like all political and religious shysters down through the ages, they ignored the facts, attacked the messengers of truth, confused the issue, and appealed to the emotions of a largely uneducated and naive populace.

These deceitful tactics worked in the first century, and they still work today, 2,000 years later! Regrettably, it is a simple fact of life that most people are much more heavily influenced by emotion, by short-term self-interest, and by rhetoric, than by truth, reason, and logic. That's political and religious reality 101!

DON'T CONFUSE ME WITH THE FACTS

To some degree or other, similar scenarios are played out daily in communities around the globe. This writer experienced two such incidents recently.

In May, 2002 he attended a dinner meeting in Vancouver, Washington, at which the guest lecturer was David Irving, the renowned British author. Irving's numerous books on World War II are all based on original documents, and may be found in leading libraries and military academies around the world. Irving is recognized as a top authority on the history of Hitler's Third Reich.

In the early minutes of his lecture Irving told how he uncovered vital historical information in both German and British archives. He explained how, over a period of years, he developed close and trusting friendships with individuals who were directly involved with German leaders during the war. These people provided him with insights and documents otherwise undiscoverable.

After some 20 minutes, his speech was most rudely interrupted. Dozens of screaming youths swarmed around the restaurant, carrying signs, pounding on the windows, screaming abuse, and chanting mindless mantras. Many had masks on. Others sported bizarre hairdos — with colors ranging from red to green to blue. At least two were identified as students at a local community (communist?) college. Another openly admitted that he, with some of his friends, had been "recruited" in Portland's Pioneer Courthouse Square. They were being paid by some unseen force for their "services."

Why was this human rabble so incensed with David Irving? Why were they so dedicated to disrupting the meeting? Why were they also hurling invective at innocent people who were exercising their constitutionally-guaranteed First Amendment right to "peaceably ... assemble"? Why the blatant lack of respect for other diners at the same restaurant?

The explanation is simple — very simple. In Toronto in 1988, David Irving was an expert witness for the defense in a trial in which the defendant was accused of defaming Jews. Irving's authoritative testimony, based on irrefutable documentation, so incensed Jewish leaders around the world that since then they have engaged in a relentless attack on his character and reputation.

The Jewish community could, of course, have exposed Irving as a liar and a false witness **had his testimony not been factual.** Refusing to debate him in an open forum, or in any other manner — and unable to disprove any of his testimony — they chose to defame his character at every turn. Frankly, this doesn't speak very favorably for **their** character and motives.

This Jewish vendetta has cost David Irving millions of dollars in royalties, speaking fees, and other forms of income.

The episode at the restaurant reminded this writer of the incident in first-century Ephesus, related earlier. When observers attempted to question some of the demonstrators regarding their motives, it was discovered that most didn't have a clue as to who David Irving was. They had never read any of his books or articles — nor seen his videos. The gathering **"was full of confusion.... Some therefore cried one thing, and some another; for the assembly was confused; and the more part knew not wherefore they were come together."**

This mindless rabble weren't interested in truth. They wouldn't recognize truth if it hit them in the face. In their *Alice in Wonderland* world of fantasy, "Nothing would be what it is. Because everything would be what it isn't. And contrary-wise, what it is, it wouldn't be. And what it wouldn't be, it would. You see?"

ISRAELI-PALESTINIAN ARTICLE

This writer's article on the historical background of the Israeli-Palestinian conflict in the April/May, 2002 issue of *Midnight Messenger* generated a lot of interest. Most was very positive, some very negative.

In a few phone calls and letters, he was charged with being against the Jews and favoring the Arabs. He was also charged with being ignorant of God's true purpose for mankind — and of God's plan that is allegedly being worked out through modern "Israel."

[Of course, nothing could be further from the truth. In years gone by, he spent endless time and energy publishing and disseminating such a false belief system. His efforts ended in spiritual burnout! When finally confronted with indisputable biblical truth, things changed!]

The conversations followed a familiar pattern. After each initial exchange, this writer asked two simple questions: Did he in any place in the article misquote, misunderstand, or misrepresent any passage of scripture? Did he at any time misquote or twist any historical facts? Was not everything he quoted right out of **their** Bibles — and right out of authentic history?

No one could dispute the fact that in each case this was true. One lady had a real gem of an "out": "But my pastor says...."

When what one's pastor says carries more authority than the Word of God, they've got a problem — **A REAL PROBLEM!** "My mind's made up, don't confuse me with the facts!"

As scripture says: "The time will come when they will not endure sound doctrine; but after their own lusts shall they heap to themselves teachers, having itching ears. **AND they shall turn away their ears from the truth, and shall be turned unto fables**" (*II Timothy* 4:3,4). Nuf said!

Turn away from the truth? What is meant by that?

WHAT DO YOU MEAN, TRUTH?

It's crucial that we again define our terms. What is rightly meant by "truth"? **And, most important of all, is there an ultimate truth?** Probably the clearest definition of the word "truth" is given by Dr. Stuart Crane in one of his seminars: "Truth is an accurate representation of the subject under consideration, (1) As it relates to **all** other things; (2) As it **always** has been in the past; (3) As it **universally** holds in the present; and (4) Shall hold **without exception** in the future. Error is **not** the opposite of truth. **Error is anything except truth. If there are any exceptions, it is error."**

There are thousands of varieties of lies, and of ways that "seem right" to people, **but there can only be one truth.** This ultimate bottom line is found in *John* 14:6. Here, Jesus Christ — the Creator and Sustainer of all things (*John* 1:1-5) — makes an awesome declaration: "I am **THE** way, **THE** truth, and **THE** life." As the Lord Jesus Christ is **THE** (singular!) way, truth, and life, is it possible that anything else can be of true, lasting value? Obviously not! Remember, "Jesus Christ [is] the same yesterday, and today, and forever" (*Hebrews* 13:8). **If Jesus Christ is telling the truth — AND HE IS — then it answers many of our questions and solves most of our problems.**

As Jesus so rightly stated, **"[T]his is the condemnation, that light is come into the world, and men loved darkness rather than light, because their deeds were evil.**

"For everyone who does evil hates the light, neither comes to the light, lest their deeds should be reproved" (*John* 3:19-20).

Today, for a multitude of reasons — not the least of which is the diabolical belief that there are no absolutes in religion, economics, and politics — few people are asking serious questions. They are not demanding answers.

Why? There is evidence that the cacophony of diabolically moronic "music" and "entertainment" with which we are all bombarded from every point of the compass is designed for the specific purpose of keeping the human mind so "busy" — and in such a state of agitation and flux — that most are rendered virtually helpless when dealing with reality. Truly, "that old serpent, called the Devil, and Satan [has] deceived the whole world" (*Revelation* 12:9).

An obvious question: **AS** Satan has deceived the **WHOLE WORLD**, which part of the world is **NOT** deceived? The answer, of course, is **NONE!** None is none! It includes not only the political, economic, and educational "worlds," **but also the world of religion!**

Right now, we are unquestionably living in a time of great religious confusion — a time of a great falling away from biblical truth. **Most churchgoers "will not endure sound doctrine."** Rejecting "**the** faith which was **once** delivered unto the saints," they have "heap[ed] to themselves teachers having itching ears." They just want to have their ears tickled by the newest religious gimmicks, the latest religious fads. They want to be made to "feel good," instead of repenting and being good. As a result, they "have turn[ed] away their ears from the truth and [are] turned unto fables" (*II Timothy* 4:4).

As explained earlier in this writer's two books *Storming the Gates of Hell* and *Biblical Insights Into God's Chosen People*, this slippery slide into apostasy began around 1830 with the dreams and visions of one, Margaret Macdonald. Over the next several decades, with the help of John Darby and Edward Irving, belief in the veracity of her hallucinations (now known as dispensationalism, or millennialism) grew very slowly. It was only with the publication of the infamous *Scofield Bible* (with its voluminous footnotes that repeatedly contradicted or twisted God's word) in the early 1900s that this heresy began to gain widespread public acceptance. This belief system is based **not** on the infallible word of God, but on the "Jewish fables, and commandments of men," warned against by Paul in *Titus* 1:14. As the Apostle warned in the same verse, they "turn [people] from the truth."

JEWISH UTOPIA

In his book *Jewish Utopia,* Rabbi Michael Higger outlines Judaism's plans for your future: "The basis of the Rabbinic Utopia is ... the millennium pictured by the prophets" (p.8). It's "a universal paradise on earth" ... a "new age" (p.25), a "new order" (p.23), "the kingdom of God" that will result in an "ideal state of social justice" (p.94). The Rabbinic Utopia will result "in the spiritual perfection of human society" (p.5).

But how about our Lord Jesus Christ? Although this planned Jewish Utopia is described as "the Messianic idea" (p.23), there is no place in it for Jesus Christ, the true Messiah. As it is allegedly "imbued with the trinity of dogmatism, prejudice, and ignorance ... Christianity will be gone" (pp.3,4). Why? In the *Babylonian Talmud*, Judaism's top authority, the Lord Jesus Christ is pictured as a bastard. It states he has no place in the world of the future. In fact, Talmudic Jews believe that Jesus (**THE** way, **THE** truth, and **THE** life) is presently boiling in excrement in hell.

As the Talmudic Jews view themselves as the world's "messiah" through Communism and Socialism (*Universal Jewish Encyclopedia*, p.548), there obviously can't be any room for Christ in the equation!

By embracing such spiritual insanity, Judeo-Christians (sic) have embraced "another gospel" — a message which perverts the gospel of Christ. It promotes "another Jesus" — one not found in **your** Bible (*Galatians* 1:6,7; *II Corinthians* 11:4). This phony "gospel" exalts the damnable heresy of a Jewish Utopia — one without the Lord Jesus Christ. As this is a false "gospel," it obviously doesn't have the explosive spiritual power of the original — the true gospel that "turned the world upside down."

Incredibly, untold millions of Christians have been conned into adopting this belief system which usurps the unique position of the Lord Jesus Christ. Like a spiritual hydrogen bomb, this heresy has decimated the physical church, causing it to splinter into innumerable factions. **Talk about apostasy!**

It is high time to awaken from our spiritual slumber "and earnestly contend for **the** faith which was **once** delivered to the saints" (*Jude* v.3). **We need to honor and glorify the Lord Jesus Christ — not those who defame him!** Jesus Christ is **THE TRUTH** which transforms — **THE TRUTH** which makes one free. He is the pivotal point of all history. He is "the Alpha and Omega, the beginning and the ending" (*Revelation* 1:8). He is "the author and finisher of our faith" (*Hebrews* 12:2). "Neither is there salvation in **any** other; for there is **none other name** under heaven given among men, whereby we must be saved" (*Acts* 4:12).

One last question: "Am I therefore your enemy because I tell you the TRUTH?" (*Galatians* 4:16). **"[L]et God be true and every man a liar"** (*Galatians* 4:3). ■

APPENDIX II

What Is the Role of Religion in the 21st Century?

By Des Griffin

Most younger Americans have been trained from kindergarten to look with disdain upon "religion." In schools, colleges, and universities they have been brainwashed into believing that religion (in this context, belief in the Bible and the existence of a Creator God who rules all things according to his will) is a fanciful myth that has held mankind in its steely grip of superstition and fear since the dawn of time. Bible-based beliefs are termed "archaic dogmas ... that inhibit creative explorations and solutions" (*Humanist Manifesto I & II*, 1933).

One highly respected educational authority, Paul Brandwein, stated that "any child who believes in God is mentally ill" (*The Social Sciences*, Harcourt Brace, 1970, p.10). That was, as we shall see, his **religious** belief!

DEFINING TERMS

As always, in order to make genuine sense of the topic at hand, we must first define our terms. Going to Noah Webster's *American Dictionary of the English Language* (1828), we find the word "religion" defined thus: "1. Religion, in its most comprehensive sense, includes a belief in the being and perfection of God, in the revelation of his will to man, in man's obligation to obey his commands, in the state of reward and punishment, and in man's accountability to God....

"**4. Any system of faith and worship. In this sense, religion comprehends the belief and worship of pagans ... any religion consisting in the belief of a superior power or powers governing the world, and in the worshiping of such power or powers....**"

FACING REALITY

In the most comprehensive sense, Americans are among the most religious people on earth. Though only a minority attend church services on a regular basis, most Americans are bombarded with religious concepts from morning till night. They get their religious "education" while attending school or college, watching the news, being amused by sitcoms on TV — or while watching the "History" Channel. They thus participate in religious activities on a regular basis.

As a result, most — **unwittingly** — have become ardently religious in their daily pursuits. They have become so zealous, in fact, that they even have their children bussed to religious temples every morning, to have their minds "topped off" with the latest religious concepts. Is it any wonder we are reaping what we have sown?

CHECKING THE FACTS

Lest the reader believe that this writer is "off the wall and out to lunch" with his observations, *let's go to the most authoritative sources and document the absolute truth of what has been stated.*

Today, the most revered religion in America is that of Humanism. In the preface of *Humanist Manifestos I and II*, we learn that "Humanism is a philosophical, **religious**, and moral point of view as old as civilization itself....

"In 1933 a group of thirty-four liberal humanists in the United States defined and annunciated the philosophical and **religious** principles that seemed to them **fundamental**.... They are intended as ... the expression of a quest for values and goals that we can work for and that can help us to take new directions....

"[Humanists] believe **[it's their religious faith!]** that traditional theism, especially faith in the prayer-hearing God, assumed to love and care for persons, to hear and understand their prayers, and to be able to do something about them, is an unproved and outmoded faith.... *Reasonable minds look for other means for survival*" [By implication, if one believes in the Creator God they have an **unreasonable mind** — and are thus **insane**].

"[The twenty-first] century can be and should be the humanistic century.... **[W]e stand at the dawn of a new age**. Using technology wisely, we can control our environment, conquer poverty, markedly reduce disease, extend our life-span, significantly modify our behavior, unlock vast new powers, and provide humankind with unparalleled opportunity for achieving an abundant and meaningful life." [Without God, man can supposedly create his own Utopia!].

"Traditional moral codes ... fail to meet the pressing needs of today and tomorrow.... They separate rather than unite people....

"Ethics is autonomous and situational, needing no theological or ideological sanction.... Happiness and the creative realization of human needs and desires ... are continuous themes of humanism. We strive for the good life, here and now" (pp.14,17). "All persons should have a voice in developing the values and goals that determine their lives" (p.19).

Humanism, **an acknowledged religion**, has been the dominant force in American society since the 1960s. Most people have been induced/seduced into accepting its diabolical tenets at face value — without any concrete proof. *It has become their religious faith.* Truly, Satan — "the god of this world" (*II Corinthians* 4:4) — "has deceived the whole world" into believing his original lie that man can be "as god" and thus create his own heaven on earth (*Revelation* 12:9; *Genesis* 3:5).

In the final analysis, have not the humanist change agents and social engineers in America's schools and colleges been enormously successful in marketing Satan's great lie that man can be "as god"? As a result, has not America been transformed from being a basically Christian nation (a fact verified on numerous occasions by the Supreme Court) into a humanistic nation? Can it not also be truthfully stated that, as a result, America has been spiritually seduced into changing its religion and its God? Humanist religious dogma decrees that man in his collective form — THE STATE — is god. This new American state god demands instant and unquestioning obedience to its every imperious utterance. And it promises to provide for those who worship and serve it from the womb to the tomb — from the cradle to the grave!

Humanists strenuously deny the natural wickedness of the human heart as revealed in Scripture. It should be noted that their efforts to change mankind through social engineering are failing abysmally. Without definite standards of right and wrong — and dynamic spiritual leadership — society is sinking into anarchy.

By the "fruit" it produces, Humanism must be identified as a destructive force.

THE MASONIC RELIGION

But how about other influential, non-Christian religious fraternities that have a major — *though usually unrecognized* — impact on American society, Freemasonry, for example? Can Masonry be relied upon to lead our country back to its spiritual roots? Let's see what true Masons believe.

A modicum of research reveals that Freemasonry is a powerful **religion,** and that its adherents hold most of the top positions in the political and judicial systems in the United States.

The fact that Masonry is truly a **religion** is openly acknowledged in their own literature. Top Masonic authority Albert Pike assures us that, **"Every Masonic lodge is a temple of religion; and its teachings are instruction in religion.... This is the true religion revealed to the ancient patriarchs**; which Masonry has taught for many centuries, and which it will continue to teach as long as time endures" (*Morals and Dogma*, pp.213-214).

Another Masonic leader, J.S.M. Ward, on page 185 of his book *Masonry: Its Aims and Ideas*, wrote: "I consider **Freemasonry as a sufficiently organized school of religion.**" Two pages later, he continued: "**Freemasonry ... has taught that each man can, by himself, work out his own conception of God,** and **thereby** achieve salvation ... it holds that there be **many paths** that lead to the throne of the all loving Father which all start from the same common source. Freemasonry believes that although these paths appear to branch off in various directions, yet **they all reach the same ultimate goal**, and that to some men one path is better and to others another."

Another high Mason — Frank C. Higgins — claims that, "It is true that **Freemasonry is the parent of all religion**" (*Ancient Freemasonry*, p.10).

Albert Pike, a former Sovereign Grand Commander of the Ancient and Accepted Rite of Freemasonry of the Southern Jurisdiction, U.S.A., tells us tells us that, "**Masonry propagates no creed except its own most simple and sublime one: that universal religion, taught by nature and by reason**" (*Morals and Dogma*, 1871, p.718).

Another top authority, Manley P. Hall, elaborates: "The **true** Mason is **not** creed-bound. He realizes with the divine **illumination** of his lodge that as a Mason **his religion** must be universal. Christ, Buddha or Mohammed, the name means little, for he recognizes only the light, not the bearer. *He worships at every shrine, bows before every altar, whether in temple, mosque, or cathedral,* realizing *with his true understanding the oneness of all spiritual truth.... No true Mason can be narrow,* for his lodge is **the divine expression of all broadness**. There is no place for little [i.e. narrow] minds in a great work" (*The Lost Keys of Freemasonry*, p.65)

What is the ultimate goal of Masonry? Henry C. Clausen, 33rd Degree Supreme Commander of the Sovereign Council, writing in *The New Age Magazine* (November, 1970) answers: "It is dedicated to bringing about the Fatherhood of God and the brotherhood of man, and the making of better men in a better world."

How can this be accomplished? J.D. Buck, in *Symbolism and Mystic Masonry*, p.57, tells us: "**Every soul must work out its own salvation**.... Salvation by faith and the vicarious atonement were **not** taught as now interpreted by Jesus, **nor** are these doctrines taught in esoteric scripture. **They are later and ignorant perversions of the original doctrines**."

Please note: salvation by works — by man's own efforts — is the central dogma around which Masonry is built. Like other forms of humanism, as quoted earlier, Masons believe that "ethics is autonomous, and situational, needing no theological or ideological sanction." In other words, "do your own thing. And make up your own rules as you go through life."

Pay particular attention to the fact that, in Masonic terms, the pure, **biblical** doctrine of salvation by grace — **NOT BY WORKS** — is an "ignorant perversion" of reality. To Masons, man — **NOT GOD** — is his own authority. There is absolutely no room for **the God of the Bible** in their ultimate worldview!

WHO IS MASONRY'S FINAL AUTHORITY?

Stop and Think! If the word of the Creator God is **not** their final authority, who or what is? And this talk about the "Fatherhood of God" and the "brotherhood of man"? How do these terms fit into the overall equation? Who is this "god" of whom they speak?

The startling — **to most** — answers come, once again, from the uppermost authorities in Masonry: Albert Pike and Manley P. Hall.

But first, we must see and recognize a vital, indispensable truth without which it is impossible to understand the religious scene at the beginning of the Third Millennium.

Sovereign Grand Commander Albert Pike tells us clearly that, **"Masonry ... conceals its secrets from all except the Adepts and Sages, or the Elect**, and *uses false explanations and misinterpretations of its symbols to mislead those who deserve only to be misled; to conceal the Truth, which it calls Light, from them, and to draw them away from it.* **Truth is not for those who are unworthy ... to receive it...."** (*Morals and Dogma*, pp.104-105).

"The Blue Degrees [lower ranks of Masonry] are but the **outer** court ... of the Temple. **Part** of the symbols are displayed there for the Initiate, **but he is intentionally misled by false interpretations**. It is **not** intended that he should understand them; but it **is** intended that he shall **imagine** he understands them. **Their true explanation is reserved for the Adepts, the Princes of Masonry**.... It is well enough for **the mass of those called Masons**, to **imagine** that all is contained in the Blue Degrees" (p.819).

What, then, is this startling Truth that is deeply concealed from all those "unworthy to receive it"? Who is the Light-bearer who guides and directs the "Adepts, the Princes of Masonry"? Once again we go to the writings of Sovereign Grand Commander Albert Pike: "Lucifer, *the Light-bearer!* .... Lucifer, the Son of the Morning! Is it *he* who bears the *Light*, and with its splendors intolerable blinds feeble, sensual, or selfish Souls? **Doubt it not!**" (p.321).

How do the Adepts, the Princes of Masonry form a close relationship with their Light-bearing god, Lucifer? In *The Lost Keys of Freemasonry*, Manley P. Hall provides the answer: Placing great emphasis on "self-mastery" and "mastery of emotion" (p.47), Hall declares: "Man can only expect to be entrusted with great power by proving his ability to use it constructively and selflessly. When the Mason learns that the key to the warrior on the block is the proper application of the dynamo of living power, he has learned the **mystery** of his Craft. **The seething powers of Lucifer are in his hands** and before he may step onward and upward, he must prove his ability to properly apply energy" (pp.47-48). This represents the heart and core of Masonry, the religion of "**the refined and reflective few**" (*Morals and Dogma*, p. 224).

It is these Luciferian "Adepts and Sages, or the Elect ... the Princes of Masons" (Pike) who are working feverishly at all levels of society — both in the United States and around the world — to bring in what they term the "Fatherhood of God and the brotherhood of man" through the establishment of a New World Order.

A top Masonic publication states that this plan is "dedicated to the unification of all races, religions and creeds. This plan, dedicated to *the new order of things*, is to make all things new — a new nation, a new race, a new civilization, and a new religion that has already been recognized and called the **'Religion of the Great Light'**" (*New Age Magazine*, September 1950, p.551). This is, of course, the modern-day version of Adam Weishaupt's Illuminati plan to create a New World Order.

This diabolical — anti-American, anti-Creator God, anti-Christian — plan is being promoted in indoctrination centers (euphemistically called schools and colleges), through the media, and through the political process. Through the teaching of evolution, multiculturalism, ecumenism, and New Age concepts — and the use of political and judicial pressure, harassment, coercion, and intimidation — most Americans are being brainwashed into surrendering their precious national heritage. America is fast becoming a socialist state that can be merged into this planned Global Plantation. Truly, these Light-bearers of Darkness have done their job very effectively.

To understand their success, we must realize that, ultimately, "**We wrestle not against flesh and blood** [mere human beings], but against principalities, against powers, against the rulers of darkness of this world, against spiritual wickedness [or wicked spirits] in high places" (*Ephesians* 6:12). These principalities and powers comprise Satan's hierarchial system of government on planet earth. Thus, in the final analysis, the forces working for the establishment of a New World Order are spiritual (Luciferian), not political, in nature. Mankind is being hoodwinked once again!

BIBLICAL CHRISTIANITY

From Colonial days, the land now known as the United States of America was deeply religious. Following the arrival of the Pilgrims at Plymouth, society in the New World was built solidly on biblical principles. As a result, John Winthrop (1588-1649) — the first governor of Massachusetts — declared: "We shall be as a city on a hill. The eyes of all people are upon us, so if we shall deal falsely with our God in this work we have undertaken and so cause Him to withdraw His present help, we shall be made a story and a by-word throughout the world."

Following the ancient Hebrews, the United States was only the second nation in history to be founded on biblical law. The Bible was the final arbiter in most disputes. Self government and personal responsibility were emphasized and practiced. The strength of early America was not based on military might. It was established firmly on the character and moral fiber of its people. Integrity, diligence, and productivity ("the protestant work ethic") were taught and practiced as a way of life. For many years strong and dynamic leaders were produced from this mold.

The Christian religion was taught in the schools and colleges. For example, Harvard University — named after John Harvard, a Puritan minister — was established in 1636 to provide highly educated leaders for the newly established Colonies. The Bible was the primary textbook. Its laws and principles formed the basis for all studies.

A century and a half later, following the establishment of the Republic, the Bible was frequently quoted as **the** authority in Congress and in the courts of the land. Its influence on the development of the nation was incalculable. The "fruit" that resulted from such an ideal environment revolutionized the world scene, turning it upside down.

Countless millions flocked to America — the new Promised Land — to enjoy the unique freedoms and opportunities it offered. The results were phenomenal. On the world scene America soon became a giant among the pygmies. The free enterprise system thus born set the stage for the amazing advances in technology that have transformed the world over the last 200 plus years.

But what has happened to America in recent decades? What factors have caused the rejection of most of the principles upon which our nation was originally built?

SUFFERING FROM BAD DOCTRINE

The spiritual condition of the American populace began to change in the mid-1800s. Again, the parallels between America and ancient Israel are striking. The massive threat that the new Bible-based Republic represented to Satan (Lucifer) is obvious. As the god — and deceiver — of the whole world (*II Corinthians* 4:4; *Revelation* 12:9), it was clear to Satan that the worldwide kingdom he was attempting to create in his own image was in jeopardy. This "thing" could spread around the globe. A massive, multi-pronged counterattack was called for.

To make headway in a society well versed in biblical doctrine, Satan, as in the first century, once again transformed himself into an "angel of light." **His** ministers were also transformed **as** the "ministers of righteousness" (*II Corinthians* 11:14,15). These agents of apostasy preached "another Jesus ... another gospel." Much of the religious terminology was the same, but the message was subverted, drastically changed. Through the agency of John Darby, Brooke Westcott, Fenton Hort, C.I. Scofield, Charles C. Finney, and numerous others, the biblically-based teachings of the early settlers were slowly subverted ["overthrown from the foundation," Webster]. The modern "prophets of Baal" became increasingly active in the new promised land. Reliance on scripture alone ("mouldy orthodoxy," Henry Ward Beecher) gave way to dependence on "spiritual" experiences and "feelings." Fast-talking con artists, claiming to preach the gospel, relied increasingly on technique, story-telling, and overt humor rather than scripture to sway their audiences. Many churchgoers were beguiled by this subtle Satanic deception and were thus "corrupted from the simplicity that is in Christ" (*II Corinthians* 11:3). No longer was the inspired word of God used exclusively as the source, (1) "for doctrine, (2) for reproof, (3) for correction, and (4) for instruction in righteousness:

"That the man of God may be perfect, **thoroughly furnished** unto all good works" (*II Timothy* 3:15-16).

Bad doctrine proliferated. New "Bibles," inspired by such spiritual reprobates as Westcott and Hort, and teaching "another Jesus" and "another gospel" became increasingly popular. Doctrine was being changed, and changed significantly for the worse.

To say that the results have been catastrophic for the Christian community is to couch the truth in the mildest possible terms. Whereas in the first century Christ's ministers, through God's word and the power of the Holy Spirit, "turned the world upside down" (*Acts* 17:6), these modern wolves in sheep's clothing have now turned the physical church upside down.

By their fruits shall you know them! Biblical Christianity was instrumental in raising America to great heights. Apostate churchianity has played a major role in undermining everything our forebears toiled so mightily to achieve.

What now? Without true spiritual leadership, America — at the beginning of the Third Millennium — finds itself, like ancient Israel, in a situation where, religiously speaking, every man does that which is right in his own eyes (See *Judges* 21:25). Confusion reigns.

Should this grim situation cause us to lose faith in the Bible as God's word? Or in Christ as redeemer, savior, and king? Absolutely not! What has happened, and is still happening, serves only to prove the marvelous accuracy of God's word. Was it not prophesied that "the time will come when they will not endure sound doctrine, but after their own lusts shall heap to themselves teachers having itching ears" (*II Timothy* 4:3)?. Is it not prophesied that "as in the days that were before the flood [of Noah] they were eating and drinking, marrying and giving in marriage, until the day that Noe entered into the ark.

"And knew not until the flood came, and took them all away; **so also shall the coming of the Son of man be**" (*Matthew* 24:38-39).

Also, "Nevertheless, when the Son of man cometh, shall he find faith on the earth?" (*Luke* 18:8). The implied answer is obviously, NO!

AMERICA HAS CHANGED ITS RELIGION

The conditions that exist today serve only to prove that, as a whole, America has changed its God. It has changed its religion. It has rejected the God of the Bible, and has gone into idolatry — worshiping everything from Lucifer to nature itself.

Most churches have been spiritually gutted. Most congregations are dying from spiritual malnutrition. There is, thank God, an elect little flock, a remnant which has not bowed the knee to Baal. They "earnestly contend for **the** faith once delivered unto the saints" (*Jude* 1:3). They are led to see — and reject — bad doctrine.

Biblical Christianity — founded by the one who is "the Way, the Truth, and the Life" (*John* 14:6) — is the only source of peace and the truly "abundant life" (*John* 10:10). Jesus Christ — **ALONE** — is The Rock (*I Corinthians* 10:4). He alone is "the author and finisher of our faith" (*Hebrews* 12:2).

All other religious faiths are vain, pointless, and futile. They are man-made, Satan-inspired forms of artificial resusitation. They thrive on falsehood and deceit. Thankfully, their author — Satan — has already been defeated (*Matthew* 4:1-10; *I Corinthians* 2:8). He, his demonic host, and their human devotees will end up in the lake of fire (*Revelation* 20:10,15).

Until judgment day, Satan's "tares" will continue to grow together with God's elect "wheat" (*Matthew* 13:24-30). In the meantime, what is Christ's admonition to his elect living in the midst of Satan's Babylonian System?: "Come out of her, **my people**, that **you** be not partakers of her sins, and that **you** receive not of her plagues" (*Revelation* 18:4).

"For where your treasure is, there will your heart be also. Let your loins be girded about, and *your* lights burning; And ye yourselves like unto men that wait for their lord, when he will return from the wedding; that when he cometh and knocketh, they may open unto him immediately. Blessed *are* those servants, whom the lord when he cometh shall find watching: verily I say unto you, that he shall gird himself, and make them to sit down to meat, and will come forth and serve them. And if he shall come in the second watch, or come in the third watch, and find *them* so, blessed are those servants" (*Luke* 12:34-38).

"Blessed is that servant, whom his lord when he comes shall find so doing" (***Matthew* 24:46**). ■

Give Copies of

Biblical Insights Into
'God's Chosen People'

To Your Friends
****

Order multiple copies at the special prices

1-2 ..... $8 each
3-5 ..... $7 each
6-9 ..... $6 each
10-20 ..... $4.50 each
50 copies ..... $4.00 each

**Please add ten percent for postage.
MINIMUM postage $5.**

Des Griffin's *Special AlertNewsletter*
Box 294 Colton OR 97017

FOURTH REICH OF THE RICH

$16.00

Des Griffin — Des Griffin takes over where other writers on the International Conspiracy leave off, bringing his readers behind the scenes in international politics and into the diabolical world of the Illuminati, the most secret of the secret societies.

In this fast moving, easy-to-read book, the author traces the history of the conspiracy down through the centuries and presents irrefutable documentation that will both shock and amaze you.

From the pages of *Fourth Reich of the Rich* pour facts that open up new vistas of knowledge and understanding. World affairs leap into life and become truly meaningful.

No wonder this book has won acclaim world wide:

"Fourth Reich is superb and should be used as a textbook in schools around the world," writes Count Sixtus von Plettenberg, economist, Germany.

"Des Griffin's book is a triumph of knowledge of his subject, clarity of thought and expression and condensation of style," Dr. Ian Anderson, Rhodesia News and World Report.

DESCENT INTO SLAVERY?

by **Des Griffin** $16.00

In a book that has been described as "devastating," "magnificent" and "superbly documented" by readers on three continents, Des Griffin zeros in on the International Bankers and presents, in carefully documented detail, the story of their involvement in the Illuminati plot to create a totalitarian One-World government.

No punches are pulled by the author as he presents startling documentation and brings his readers face-to-face with the raw realities of power politics.

Here, at last, is the full, true story of the power-crazed Internationalists and the methods they employ in steering all nations towards total social and financial ruin in preparation for their ultimate absorption into the planned worldwide dictatorship. The inside story behind World War II is truly eye-opening!

Des Griffin lays bare the hideous tragedy that lies ahead for the United States unless our people shake off the shackles of the conspirators and return to individual responsibility and fiscal sanity.

This is one book you can't afford to miss!

Des Griffin's Books
****

Fourth Reich of the Rich
and
Descent Into Slavery?

Order either or both books
at the following prices:

1-2 copies $16 each
3-5 copies $13 each
6-9 copies $11 each
10-19 copies $10 each
20-29 copies $9 each.
30 copies or more $8 each

Please add 10% for shipping. MINIMUM $5.

Des Griffin's Special Alert Newsletter
Box 294 Colton OR 97017

Phone: (503) 824-2050

Name..
Address..
City.................... State......... Zip................

ANTI-SEMITISM: AND THE BABYLONIAN CONNECTION

$8.00

Des Griffin — ANTI-SEMITISM. That word strikes stark terror into the hearts and minds of many. Most will go to practically any length to avoid being smeared as "anti-Semitic."

Who is a Semite? Are all Jews Semites? What IS anti-Semitism? Is Judaism the God-centered religion of the Old Testament? What is Pharisaism? How important is the Babylonian Talmud to modern Jews? How did the Talmud come into being? What does it teach regarding Jews — and non-Jews?

Are those people who ask ANY valid questions regarding the Jews and Judaism, wicked, nasty and evil — and worthy of being ostracized, socially?

Des Griffin believes that all these questions — and more — must be addressed honestly and freely in an open forum.

Delving into biblical and secular history, and a wide variety of Jewish sources stretching back more than 2400 years, Des Griffin has come up with a truly enthralling book — one that is exciting, explosive, revealing and educational! This book will CHALLENGE you. It will make you think about — and ponder — many factors you may previously have been unaware of.

ANTI-SEMITISM: And The Babylonian Connection is a book for TODAY. It addresses the issues of today head on. It is packed with thoroughly documented facts, with insights and understanding that will give you a totally new perspective on the world in which we live.

STORMING THE GATES OF HELL
By Des Griffin $14.00

In this book, Des Griffin goes further than ever before in exposing the diabolical forces behind today's chaotic world scene. He also provides his readers with the wonderfully exhilarating answers to those conditions.

Storming the Gates of Hell is the culmi-nation of some 50 years of in-depth research. From its pages pour insights, commentary, and truths combined and put together with vivid clarity and depth of understanding.

Are you wondering how the jumbled and apparently unintelligible maze of world history could possibly make any sense and logic as we begin another millennium? As you read this book, all the pieces of the fascinating global jigsaw puzzle will fall into place in a thrilling manner; it will hold you in its grip from start to finish.

Are you turned off by religion? Are you sick and tired of the phony baloney that passes for Christianity on TV and radio — and in your own neighborhood church? If so, you need to read this book.

Condensed and focused, *Storming the Gates of Hell* is an easy-to-read, easy-to-understand book that puts history — politics, religion, secret societies, and Christianity — in proper perspective. There is real hope for the future following the **Big Showdown** between **good** and **evil**.

MARTIN LUTHER KING
THE MAN BEHIND THE MYTH

By Des Griffin $7.00

The late Dr. Martin Luther King continues to be very much in the news. In 1983, Congress decreed that a National Holiday be established in honor of the late civil rights leader. Nationwide, hundreds of cities have renamed streets, parks, schools, convention centers and freeways in honor of King. In death, Martin Luther King has become much more popular than when he was alive.

From coast-to coast, voices are raised in protest over this national glorification of King. They are asking serious questions that cry out for answers.

In political circles, and in the media, these voices are roundly condemned as being racist, bigoted, and narrow-minded, if not altogether Neanderthal. Any criticism of King is said to be part of a smear campaign, and thus beneath contempt.

What type of individual was the late Martin Luther King? Was he a saint, or a man of questionable character? Was he dedicated to improving the lot of black people, or was he marching to the beat of a different drum? What motivated him? What was his educational background? Who was behind him? Who financed him?

What was King's personal philosophy? Was his personal life exemplary, befitting a preacher of the gospel? Or did King have what J. Edgar Hoover described as "the morals of a tom cat"?

Was King assassinated in cold blood by the late James Earl Ray? Or was Ray the unwitting victim of a much deeper plot that reached into the highest echelons of the federal government?

These are a few of the questions asked — and answered — by Des Griffin in his book, *Martin Luther King: The Man Behind the Myth*. This fascinating book is packed with carefully documented details about King's life — and death. Des Griffin lays bare the facts in an easy-to-read, easy-to-understand style that will hold you from start to finish.

9 780941 380089

Printed by Libri Plureos GmbH in Hamburg, Germany